"SWEEPING and INSIGH[...]"

One of the definitive acco[...]
Central American [...]
—Manuel Roig-Franzia, [...]

"Urgent and propulsive... Makes a persua[...]
from US foreign policy in Central America to t[...] crisis."
—*The New York Times*

EVERYONE WHO IS GONE IS HERE

A NATIONAL BESTSELLER

THE UNITED STATES, CENTRAL AMERICA, AND THE MAKING OF A CRISIS

JONATHAN BLITZER

Now in paperback

From *New Yorker* staff writer Jonathan Blitzer

An epic, heartbreaking, and deeply reported history of the disastrous humanitarian crisis at the southern border told through the lives of the migrants forced to risk everything and the policymakers who determine their fate

 PenguinPress | www.prh.com/everyonewhoisgoneishere

GRANTA

12 Addison Avenue, London W11 4QR | email: editorial@granta.com
To subscribe visit subscribe.granta.com, or call +44 (0)1371 851873

ISSUE 170: WINTER 2025

EDITOR	Thomas Meaney
MD & DEPUTY EDITOR	Luke Neima
SENIOR EDITOR	Josie Mitchell
MANAGING EDITOR	Tom Bolger
ASSOCIATE DESIGN DIRECTOR	Daniela Silva
ASSOCIATE EDITOR	Brodie Crellin
EDITORIAL ASSISTANT	Aea Varfis-van Warmelo
PHOTOGRAPHY EDITOR	Max Ferguson
COMMERCIAL DIRECTOR	Noel Murphy
OPERATIONS & SUBSCRIPTIONS	Sam Lachter
MARKETING	Simon Heafield
PUBLICITY	Pru Rowlandson, publicity@granta.com
CONTRACTS	Margaux Vialleron
ADVERTISING	Renata Molina-Lopes, Renata.Molina-Lopes@granta.com
FINANCE	Suzanna Carr
SALES	Rosie Morgan
IT SUPPORT	Mark Williams
PRODUCTION & DESIGN DIRECTOR	Sarah Wasley
PROOFS	Katherine Fry, Gesche Ipsen, Jessica Kelly, Jess Porter, Will Rees, Francisco Vilhena
CONTRIBUTING EDITORS	Anne Carson, Rana Dasgupta, Michael Hofmann, A.M. Homes, Rahmane Idrissa, Karan Mahajan, George Prochnik, Leo Robson, Janique Vigier
PUBLISHER	Sigrid Rausing

p.5 This introductory quote is taken from *The Love of Singular Men*, released in 2023 by Peirene Press Ltd and first published in Brazil under the Portuguese-language title *O amor dos homens avulsos* by Companhia das Letras © 2016 by Victor Heringer; p.43 Quotes an excerpt from *Power, Money & Sex: How Success Almost Ruined My Life* by Deion Sanders. Copyright © 1999 by Word Publishing. Used by permission of HarperCollins Christian Publishing; p.98 Excerpt from *England, England* by Julian Barnes, copyright © 1998 by Julian Barnes. Used by permission of Alfred A. Knopf, an imprint of the Knopf Doubleday Publishing Group, a division of Penguin Random House LLC. All rights reserved.

IN *BRICK* 114

NATALIE DIAZ
CLAIRE MESSUD
DEBORAH LEVY
AMITAVA KUMAR
VICTORIA CHANG
ROBERT BRINGHURST
JOANNA BIGGS
KYO MACLEAR
JOSÉ TEODORO
KAYAL VIZHI
JANA OMAR ELKHATIB
GREG HOLLINGSHEAD
LUCY IVES
JAKE KENNEDY
KENZIE ALLEN
HEBE UHART
ELIOT WEINBERGER

Order the latest issue
at BRICKMAG.COM

@BRICKLITERARY

CONTENTS

Imagine God's tiredness on the eighth day, right after inventing this race of seed-spillers, this race of conquistadors and record-breakers, of Himalayan mountaineers, men and women who build the biggest houses of cards, pull trucks with their ears, construct the tallest buildings and start the biggest snowball fights in history and then they die. Then they die, the morons!

–Victor Heringer, *The Love of Singular Men*

Introduction

*I*t's not whether you win or lose, it's how you play the game. Any schoolchild can smell the rat in the adage. The great thing about sports, we are told, is that they teach the virtues of comradeship, perseverance, humility, respect for rules – 'sportsmanship'. But everybody knows a game is not worth watching unless the players are trying to win – unless someone is willing to risk the high tackle, smash the serve, steal the base, or throw the knock-out punch.

For the post-religious, games are one of the few means of experiencing redemption and a degree of transcendence amid the sleepwalking called 'living'. Sports promise meaning, delivered within a fixed amount of time. They have clear stakes, characters with strengths and flaws, and there is the chance of witnessing something unforgettable. In this, sports shares some of the narrative features of stories, which may be why they have always been such a natural subject for them. Homer's heroes in the *Iliad* exhibit a larger range of emotions – giddiness, sadness, frustration, satisfaction – during the funeral games of Patroclus than they do on the battlefield.

There are always purifying factions who want to clean up games, to save players from themselves. In the nineteenth century, Jeremy Bentham targeted a villainous behavior he called 'deep play' – games with stakes so high no rational person would engage in them. The trouble is that it's only when performances are most 'irrational', when they dispense with ordinary calculation, that they become sublime. Simone Biles going for broke on the balance beam when a standard routine could still bring her the gold; Larry Bird shooting for three when a simple lay-up would be enough; Michael Jordan viciously taunting his rivals for not playing their best.

The language of winning that suffuses the modern business world often seems like a way of obscuring its more mundane character. We are meant to hail Elon Musk like some combination of Albert Einstein and Babe Ruth for channeling government subsidies toward electronic vehicles and privatizing other public goods. The imperatives of such unheroic competition are embedded in the lives of even the smallest citizens. Outside the *Granta* office on Holland Park Avenue, you can hear tiny besuited English schoolchildren comparing their exam results, lamenting any ground given in the race of CV-burnishing they seem doomed to run for the rest of their lives. Yet there is an unmistakable mix of magic and aggression in the air when children dream up and argue over games with elaborate rules of their own making, a capacity most lose as they grow older, but which seem to contain the seeds of culture and art. As Jean Baudrillard observed, the reduction of play to the level of function – play as therapy, play as school, play as catharsis, play as creativity – is the opposite of the 'passion for illusion' that once characterized its seductive power.

This issue of *Granta* returns to sports writing, which once featured often and prominently in our pages. In 1993, the magazine gave over nearly a whole issue to the poet Ian Hamilton's meditations on the English midfielder Paul Gascoigne, 'Gazza Agonistes'. Hamilton knew he had stumbled upon a special quarry. '[Gazza] was always looking to nutmeg defenders when it would have been easier to pass them by,' he wrote. 'He wanted the ball *all the time:* for throw-ins, free kicks, corners – goal-kicks, if they had let him.' In contrast to most sports commentary, which sounds like an exercise of lobbing clichés back and forth, we believe sports *writing* is an exalted literary form which has seen some worthy match-ups over time: C.L.R. James on cricket, Joyce Carol Oates on Mike Tyson, John Updike on Ted Williams, David Foster Wallace on Roger Federer, J.M. Coetzee on rugby, John Jeremiah Sullivan on the Kentucky Derby.

The 'Winners' issue features the poet Declan Ryan on the heavyweight fight between Anthony Joshua and Daniel Dubois at Wembley stadium last September. Ryan not only registers the bloodlust of the spectators, the way the boxing industry treats competitors like commodities, the psychology and ingredients of the triumph in the ring, the agony of defeat, but also the emptiness of victory, when the winner can declare nothing but a canned line from the film *Gladiator*, 'Are you not entertained?' In her piece on the history and evolution of tennis, Clare Bucknell shows how the rules of a sport can shift over time to reflect a society's values as much as its laws. Bucknell recounts her experience touring and playing a vestigial version of the game – the result of an eighteenth-century schism – that still has passionate players and courts around the globe.

'Winning isn't everything; it's the only thing,' is a line attributed – it should perhaps not surprise us – to an American college football coach in a locker room in 1950. 'Red' Sanders was a product of US military academies, who had recently returned from the Second World War, and led the UCLA Bruins to a national championship three years later. As Nico Walker writes in this issue, president Teddy Roosevelt thought of football as useful conditioning to ready men grown slack from *doux commerce* for the hard business of war. He tells how the changing vocabulary of the battlefield – cavalry metaphors in the 1910s, aerial bombing metaphors in the 1940s – testified to the tight compact between war and sport. 'When you were kids,' General George Patton told the US Third Army in 1944, 'you all admired the champion marble shooter, the fastest runner, the big-league ball players and the toughest boxers. Americans love a winner and will not tolerate a loser . . . I wouldn't give a hoot in hell for a man who lost, and laughed.'

If Jim Thorpe was the all-around star of football before the Second World War, the stars in the later decades, Jim Brown and Deion Sanders and others, could no longer afford to sidestep the spectacle of hype as the game became more mercilessly marketized, to the point that winning itself fades in significance. 'What is the college coach's priority,' Walker asks, 'to win a championship or to try to get as many players as possible into the pros?'

War has its own properties. The period of European history of the *Kabinettskriege* – wars fought according to agreed rules of engagement, and with the minimal involvement of civilians – may be mostly mythical. But the more comprehensive victories celebrated by winning states in recent memory have often been more devastating, and often less stable than they appear. The end of the Cold War left smoldering dissatisfactions on the continent that almost any Russian leadership would try one day or another to correct. Likewise, Israel's recent military successes in Gaza, Lebanon and Syria suggest a war that has gone better than its architects could have expected, but at the cost of arousing an alarming amount of international enmity, and dispensing in the process with the last tattered fig leaf of the 'liberal international order'. In photography by An-My Lê and Myriam Boulos we see both sides of that order in action: the US military operations around the globe, and migrant laborers from Sierra Leone in Beirut, who have endured a cruelly compounded calamity, first as rightless workers in Lebanon's kafala system, second as refugees bombed out of their places of employment by Israeli forces.

The fiction in this issue includes two pairs of stories: compact, dreamlike sequences by Caryl Churchill and Kathryn Scanlan from either side of the Atlantic, with Churchill finely attuned to the absurd, and Scanlan playing with the dilation of impressions. And there are two stories set in hospitals: Benjamin Nugent's 'Round One' is a comic account of reproductive woe and moral hubris that carries on the American tradition of Wallace and Saunders, while K Patrick's 'Appendix' is a story of a medical doctor who looks to redress some of the ways her professional commitment has crowded out other elements of her character. Set in an archipelago infested with angels, the Romanian writer Mircea Cărtărescu presents the reader with an inscrutable portal to another world, and Edward Salem invites us on nights out in the West Bank filled with heat and lust and rage.

Our next issue will be dedicated to 'Dead Friends', and in the autumn *Granta* will return to India for its third special issue devoted to the country. ∎

TM

DAVID SALLE
Angels in the Rain, 1998
DACS

A GOOD DAY

Caryl Churchill

The day didn't start well. I was going to be evicted for non-payment of rent and I had a fight with my girlfriend.

I said Why don't you put the lids back on jars properly so they don't come off when I pick them up?

She said You think you're so political but it's all just meaningless crap.

I said I don't really think your paintings are any good, I just say that to make you feel ok.

She said Of all the people I've slept with you're the most dull.

I said I wish we were both dead.

She said Goodbye.

I sat there a while. I sat there a long while.

Right, I said to myself, I'll go out.

Walking down the street I checked my phone. I had an email telling me I'd got the job. I'd got the job. I wouldn't be evicted. I'd begin to get somewhere.

I wanted to tell my girlfriend but I didn't.

I kept on walking. The sun was out.

I decided to go and see my friend whose brother just died in an accident. He was on holiday in France and he fell off a roof.

I said Is it ok just turning up?

He said The thing is he's in heaven.

Ok I said.

I don't feel too bad he said because it must have been very quick and of course he's in heaven now, he's in bliss and he wasn't when he was alive. And I do miss him but life's quite short anyway so I'll soon see him again.

Do you feel you're in touch with him? I said.

Yes he said he's watching over me just like when we were little and he was my big brother.

That's great I said, that's amazing.

Yes I'm surprised myself how ok it is he said.

I went on down the street. I saw a homeless man I sometimes give money to.

He said Hey good news. I'm getting housed. Not in a hostel, I've got a flat.

Very good news I said. How did that happen?

Haven't you heard he said there's a new government policy, get people off the streets by next week, double universal credit and build thousands of low-rent council flats. Oh and stop rich foreigners buying up places and not living in them.

I said What? Really?

Yes he said it's a complete turnaround. Like the boats.

What's with the boats? I said.

They're going to let most people stay he said. They'll have a proper system. I don't know the detail but check it out. And I hate to ask he said but

So I gave him the change in my pocket and on I went.

My phone rang. Was it my girlfriend? No.

My friend said Guess what? About my brother.

What's happened? I said.

Turns out he's ok he said. He didn't die at all.

I said Wow how that's amazing news.

He said Yeah, seems he was just knocked out and his friends panicked and sent the wrong message, he just broke his leg but not badly, he's completely fine.

I said So he's not in heaven.

No he said but this is better.

Of course I said. You can both be in heaven later.

Exactly he said.

So the day was looking up. I went to the park. I liked the bare branches. The clouds and blue sky were rushing through.

I suddenly had one of those I can't find words for it one of those moments of joy I suppose it is.

One of those.

They don't last but they're good when they happen.

I went to see my mother. I hadn't been for a while and she's not well. I didn't mention about my girlfriend.

She said I've got some news. I had a scan result this morning and the cancer's gone.

Gone? I said. Like in remission?

They said there's no trace of it she said. It's not at all likely to come back.

I gave her a hug. I picked up her favourite vase and waved it in the air and shouted.

She said Careful with that. She said Thinking about dying and my life I thought about ways I failed you.

I said You didn't.

She said Of course I did. Like when you had chickenpox and I was working and you were looked after by the neighbour with the scary dog.

I said I wasn't scared of the dog.

Well she said lots of small things and I'm sorry. Just let me know any time if you're feeling wronged.

Thank you I said. I don't expect I'll need to.

I just thought I'd say she said.

We were having a cup of tea and a biscuit and the news was on.

The news said Israel had stopped bombing Gaza and pulled out of the West Bank. There was going to be a big reconciliation and a complete rethink.

I was speechless.

My mother said That's another then.

What? What else? I said.

You must have heard about Ukraine she said. They've stopped fighting and they're sorting it out. And I think there's something about Darfur. Everyone seems to be changing their attitude she said. Like they've cancelled the poor countries' debts. It's a complete change in the world economy and we can stop worrying about the climate.

I nearly dropped my mug and I grabbed at it and my elbow caught the vase and it flew up in the air and I reached for it with my right hand but knocked it sideways and I went down low and knocked it up with my left hand and it went up in the air again and on its way down my mother caught it.

She said That was lucky because it's really fragile. I love that vase.

By the time I got home it was getting dark. I missed my girlfriend. She was the one I wanted to talk to about all the things that were happening. I picked up the phone and she walked in the door.

She said I'm sorry.

I said No I'm sorry.

She said I just get upset and say stuff.

I said I do like your paintings really.

She said I know they're not good, I just like doing them.

I said I like looking at them.

She said And obviously I love making love with you.

I said I don't want to die after all and who cares about the lids of jars?

Why don't we just get married and have kids? she said.

I said Yes. I said I was thinking that too.

Later on I said But what about –?

We'll work it out she said.

I said ok.

So it turned out to be quite a good day. ∎

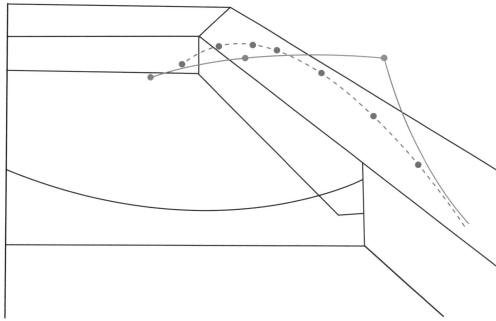

Tennis court at Hardwick House, 1896
Historic England Archive

REAL TENNIS

Clare Bucknell

Real tennis courts are like secrets. Unless you know they exist, it's hard to stumble upon them. Often, they hide in plain sight. There is something very pleasing about walking through the gates of former royal palaces – Hampton Court, the Château de Fontainebleau near Paris – and knowing you won't be stopped because you're carrying a wooden racket. Other courts are more tucked away. In upstate New York, the Tuxedo Club, founded in 1886 by playboy and tobacco heir Pierre Lorillard IV, stands behind locked park gates, atop a series of winding roads flanked by vast Gilded Age piles. Thousands of miles away in rural Victoria, about an hour's drive inland from Melbourne, there is a court nestled among the vineyards at a winery in the Macedon Ranges. You can play real tennis inside a private Catholic university in New Jersey, or on courts fronted by unassuming timber-clad cafes in the Basque region of France. The Racquet Club in downtown Philadelphia houses a real tennis court, the first swimming pool in the country constructed above ground level, and a full-size German beer hall.

Somewhere in the countryside by the River Thames, down a little track sandwiched between paddocks and flooded fields, sits Hardwick House Tennis Club. The club is attached to a sprawling Victorian red-brick house that is rumoured to have inspired Kenneth

Grahame's Toad Hall. In 1896, Joseph Bickley, a master builder who oversaw the construction of several real tennis courts across Britain and the United States, built one at Hardwick for the landowner, Sir Charles Rose. Finding it slightly too far to walk from his house, Rose demanded another. (The original building, derelict and open-roofed, is still visible from the narrow drive as you approach.) Inside, Hardwick is ferociously cold, even in summer, so players arrive wrapped up and ready to light the fire in the dining room. Dogs toast themselves in front of it or bark at the sight of loose balls. The court is large, high-roofed and echoey, with a slippery, terracotta-coloured floor and slate-grey walls showing the blotches made by balls and sweaty palms.

I first played at Hardwick at a tournament about ten years ago. On the train up from London, a stranger spotted the long handle of my racket and introduced himself; it turned out he was heading to the same place. We were given a lift from the station in an open-top sports car and handed Bloody Marys (non-virgin, non-negotiable) on arrival. This, I learned, was the way things were done. Showing up with a sports drink or a banana would have been a faux pas; likewise refusing the cocktail or trying to get out of having pudding until after playing. At Hardwick, trying too hard is frowned upon. Undue physical exertion is held to be inelegant. 'Is she running?' I remember one opponent asking incredulously, as I flung myself, sweating, after a ball.

I discovered real tennis – the historical precursor to the sport played at Wimbledon and Roland Garros – by chance at Oxford, assigned one afternoon to shepherd a group of summer-school students to a trial session. We arrived at a small, white-painted building in the heart of town, which I'd walked past roughly daily for the previous half-decade and never given a second thought. I had played tennis since childhood and a lot of squash; I assumed this would be a mixture of the two and that I'd pick it up easily enough. It was humbling to discover that it was unlike either: or, more accurately, that it combined the hardest bits of both, with elements of hockey and billiards thrown in for good measure. The ball dropped like a stone, the racket's sweet spot was minuscule, and trying to read a shot spinning off the walls was like being asked to decipher a line of code at high speed. For a long time, I was hopeless, foxed by everything. A man in his nineties who could barely move but had a devilish serve trounced me regularly. Frustration and humiliation drew me in, as they do many obsessive types. A friend who played tennis for the Netherlands in the 1980s, making it to the second round of Roland Garros, got thrashed 6–0, 6–0 in his first real tennis match and never looked back.

Modern-day tennis, the sport we all know, has a surprisingly short history. In 1874, Walter Clopton Wingfield, a retired army major, secured the patent for an outdoor ball game he called 'sphairistiké' (botched Greek for 'the game of ball'). The new sport could be played on any decently sized patch of mown grass or croquet lawn and was considered decorous enough for women to take part. Soon to be renamed 'lawn tennis', it took off because it was straightforward and accessible: all you needed were rackets, rubber balls, a makeshift net, and some paint or tape to mark lines. Wingfield marketed boxed sets of equipment for five guineas and sold more than a thousand between the summers of 1874 and 1875. Soon, rival enthusiasts came forward with their own versions of the new racket game; rival manufacturers, picking up on the key features, produced pirate equipment sets. In 1877, in an effort to pin down what the sport was about, a commission at the All England Lawn Tennis and Croquet Club laboriously formalised the rules. On 9 July, the first ball was served at a tournament in Wimbledon.

The fact that something called 'tennis' had existed long before 'lawn tennis' created a problem. Those who clung to the older sport, a game dating from the medieval period, saw the new version as an interloper and felt the threat of extinction. They engaged in a swift rebranding exercise: what they played was not tennis but real tennis, the real thing, the authentic game. 'I believe you occasionally play tennis, I mean "real" tennis?' an interviewer asked the German lawn tennis champion Victor Voss in 1900.

For years, I believed that the 'real' in 'real tennis' referred to its royal heritage. 'No, real as in royal. You know, like Real Madrid,' I'd say smugly if anyone asked. (Usually a variation on: 'You play *real* tennis? What, as opposed to *fake* tennis?') In fact, the obvious meaning of the word is the right one. As Wingfield's newfangled game took off in Britain, France, Germany, and the United States (one 1898 French book called it, not unkindly, *le bâtard*), men and women who preferred duking it out on Gothic-looking indoor courts with slippery stone floors stuck an adjective in front of what they were playing. 'Real tennis' was born, or born again.

The way real tennis is played now, by about 4,000 active players on approximately fifty surviving and new-built courts in Britain, France, the US, and Australia, has changed little since the early modern period. Like lawn tennis, it is played on a double-ended court divided by a net. Like squash, it is played indoors and players can hit the ball off the walls to create angles and spin (a type of shot known as a 'boast'). The serving player opens the game by sending the ball onto a sloping roof (the 'penthouse') that runs along the length of the court to her left. Her opponent waits at the opposite end (the 'hazard side') and may either volley the ball or wait for it to bounce. The goal of both players is either to hit one of several point-scoring targets dotted around the court (more on those later), or to force their opponent to make an error – to miss the ball, hit it into the net, or put it out of bounds.

In lawn tennis, if a player is unable to reach a ball before it bounces twice, she loses the point. In real tennis, a double-bounce doesn't automatically mean a lost point. Instead, an ancient and complicated set of rules known as the 'chase system' comes into operation. Players must take note of the spot where the ball bounced the second time. If it landed four yards from the back of the court, for example, a chase of 'four' is called. (Numbered lines painted on the walls and floor help to mark the yardage.) The chase is then held in reserve ('banked'), until the game score reaches forty or another chase – a second double-bounce point – occurs in the same game. As soon as one of these things happens, the players switch ends. The player now at the receiving end must 'beat the chase' – that is, she must play a shot which, if her opponent fails to get to it before the second bounce, will land nearer to the back wall than the original ball. Given our chase of 'four', a ball whose second bounce fell three yards from the back of the court, or two, would win the point. Are you still with me here?

Precision, rather than power, is key. If you are the sort of person who likes to smack the ball (I'm guilty of this myself), you have to try and fight your instincts, because an overhit shot will ricochet off the back wall and land, most likely, past that original four-yard mark – at five yards, say, or six – which will lose you the point. Subtler shots, 'stroked' or 'cut' into the corners using slice, are the holy grail. There is also an element of what you might call negative capability. In most sports, you're conditioned to hit every ball you can. In real tennis, one of the hardest things is learning to leave certain balls. Let's say your opponent, aiming to beat a chase of 'four', instead plays a shot that you know will land beyond it, at 'six'. You win the point by allowing the ball to bounce twice. For months, as a novice, I was unable to fathom this. Sometimes my brain would kick into gear ('DON'T HIT IT!') and sometimes it wouldn't. But even when it did, my body wouldn't obey. Time after time, I would move, reach out, hit the ball, let my opponent off the hook.

The less complicated way to score a point is to hit one of a number of targets built into the court. These are known as 'openings', because they resemble windows or doors. Here we come to the question of what a real tennis court looks like. (An average court, that is, because all courts vary slightly, with different dimensions and roof angles and floor speeds – another complicating factor.) Trying to describe one is a bit like trying to describe a duck-billed platypus, in that it wouldn't make much sense even if you were standing in front of it. At the receiving end is the 'grille', a small, rectangular opening that looks like a blocked-up window and makes a satisfying sound when you hit it. Behind the server, a large opening resembling a football net, called the 'dedans', serves as a target for the receiver. The 'winning gallery', the most challenging opening to hit, is fitted with a set of bells that chime when struck. (In Newmarket, the bells make the sound of horseshoes, appropriately for the home of horse racing.) To make everyone's job a bit harder, there is a slanting buttress in front of the grille called the 'tambour', off which the ball glances unpredictably.

A point that involved all of these elements might go something like this. Let's imagine the server employs a 'railroad', one of many possible serves, to put the ball into play. Her opponent, at the hazard end, hits a powerful return (a 'force'), aiming to send the ball into the dedans, but the server has clocked this and manages to block it in time on the volley. Her volley, aiming for the grille, instead ricochets off the tambour; the receiving player scrambles for it and slides the ball into the opposite back corner, aiming to create a chase. The server is too quick for her and manages to whip a forehand cross-court into the winning gallery. Point over. Thunderous applause.

Spectators – sometimes quiet and well behaved, sometimes loud, partisan, and tipsy – sit directly behind the dedans netting, at a safe distance. Markers, who keep score and call the chases, also sit here during matches, perched on high stools. The braver among them stand just inside the court by the net, ducking as serves whistle over their heads. It's a fun quirk of the sport that because of its size, it can support only a limited number of professional players, which means that the club pros who mark your games and help you with your backhand are often among the best in the world – like Novak Djokovic watching patiently and saying 'fifteen–love' as you fluff an easy ball.

The smallness of the sport is reflected in the kinds of people who play. Real tennis attracts eccentrics like moths to a flame. Clubs can feel like clinics: everyone you encounter has something slightly wrong with them, usually in a benign way. The demographic is small – it sometimes seems as if half the players are middle-aged men called Simon or John – but it is steadily growing. (Years ago, there

were men who would ask 'Whose wife are you?' when I showed up
to matches with my racket and full kit, but they seem to be less in
evidence these days.) 'Realers' people are also more likely than most
to have extremely strange jobs, or no jobs. One man I got chatting
to at a dinner at Queen's Club was involved in some way with South
African mines. He offered to cut me in; I said yes politely and hoped
he wouldn't remember. Another claimed to have introduced the sport
of padel to the Americas.

The game survives through the efforts of enthusiastic individuals
and a culture of near-heroic generosity. During tournaments, locals
often host travelling players, offering 'billets' for the night like civilians
putting up soldiers during the Second World War. In Tuxedo Park, I
once reversed a hired SUV into our host's ornamental rock garden
and had to slip out at night to rearrange the stones. On another
occasion, a man I barely knew offered to lend me his vintage Jaguar
to drive myself back and forth to the club. The conviviality goes hand
in hand with intense competitiveness. Players who were seen necking
champagne into the early hours arrive on court at 8.30 a.m., whey-
faced but determined. At the Royal Melbourne Tennis Club a few
years ago, during a hard-fought doubles tournament, a group of
ferocious older women had to be officially cautioned for chanting
'KILL! KILL! KILL!' from the dedans.

R eal tennis players like to say that theirs is the only proper racket
sport because the rest aren't difficult enough. Many see it as an
intrinsically noble game, a 'sport of kings'. Henry VIII, one of history's
sportiest royals, played it to a high standard. Not to be outdone, his
rival Francis I of France had a tennis court installed on his battleship,
the *Grande Françoise*. Henry VII played, though less well. Henry V
is likely to have played too. There is a bit in Shakespeare's *Henry V*
– apparently without a basis in fact – in which the French dauphin
sends Henry a barrel of tennis balls as an insult, prompting Henry to
declare (using fiery tennis metaphors) that he will crush the French
and defend his ancient claim to French lands. In the medieval period,

kings seemed to make a habit of dying from tennis, either through violent quarrels or overexertion or extreme bad luck. In 1498, Charles VIII of France fatally smacked his forehead on a lintel while trying to show his consort, Anne of Brittany, a match played in the castle moat. A very brilliant story tells us that James I of Scotland perished in 1437 after leaping into a privy to escape a band of conspirators; he was murdered because he had ordered the privy's exit to be bricked up, to prevent his tennis balls rolling into it from the court next door.

Lurid tales like these tend to obscure the fact that tennis began as a game for ordinary people. Plenty of them came to grief over it, but fewer of their stories survive. We know about one nasty altercation in Antwerp in 1567: a man named Pieterssen stabbed his opponent, Van Scherus, the local tennis professional, to death, after Van Scherus hit a ball under the net cord and refused to admit it. The earliest surviving mentions of tennis, or of a game recognisably close to it, come from mid-twelfth-century France, in documents describing the pastimes of the provincial clergy. They indicate that monks and clerks, having been banned by the Church authorities from joining in the local rowdy football matches, sought an alternative closer to home. The stone arches around monastic cloisters were similar enough to the goals used in football to make a new game possible: teams of players would face each other, one team defending the arched opening, or 'goal', while the other attacked it. Special features of the cloisters, such as the grille, or barred window through which monks communicated with laymen outside, supplied additional target areas.

Instead of kicking the ball with their feet, players began experimenting with hitting it with their bare or gloved hands, either on the bounce or in the air. Over time, the *jeu de paume*, or 'game of the palm', as tennis was first known, developed, spreading from the provinces to Paris, then to Flanders and eventually across Western Europe. In France, it continued to be known as the *jeu de paume* even after gut-strung rackets began to be adopted in court circles in the early sixteenth century. Modern rackets reflect this aspect of the game's origins. Like the human hand, they are asymmetrical rather than perfectly oval, with a rounded side (mirroring the curve of the thumb) and a flattened bottom. Among players with working knees, there is pride in being able to lunge low enough to the ground to strike the ball such that the flat side grazes the floor.

The clergy soon lost its de facto monopoly over the early game. In 1450, the Dean of Exeter denounced a group of youths from the town who had overrun the cathedral cloisters to play tennis, 'defowl[ing]' the walls and smashing the glass windows. Sons of the aristocracy, sent to monasteries for their education, learned one important lesson: there was now a game called *jeu de paume* and cloisters were essential to play it. On feudal estates, as early as the thirteenth century, there was a sudden and suspicious spike in the number of ecclesiastical building projects. The newly founded 'monasteries' were fragmentary, often left with half a cloister – the minimum architecture required for a game.

Commoners, meanwhile, played in the streets and on town squares, sometimes negotiating with neighbours for the privilege of using their gable walls as playing surfaces. 'You may commonly see artisans, such as hatters and joiners, playing at tennis for a crown,' a sixteenth-century Frenchman reported from England. Sir Robert Dallington, a courtier who travelled in France during the 1590s, noted that French children played well and women too: 'ye would think they were born with Rackets in their hands'. The most touching evidence of tennis's broad appeal is perhaps the fact that in the *Second Shepherds' Play*, part of a mystery cycle performed by local people in Yorkshire in the fifteenth and sixteenth centuries, the baby Jesus receives an unexpected gift: a tennis ball. 'Hail, hold forth thy hand small; I bring thee but a ball,' the Third Shepherd tells him gently. 'Have thou and play withal, / And go to the tennis.'

For centuries, the authorities did their best to stamp the game out. Medieval prelates disliked the idea of monasteries becoming hubs of rowdy gameplay. In 1451, the Bishop of Exeter summarily excommunicated a group of canons belonging to the parish of Ottery St Mary: they had been playing 'an evil game called tennis' in the churchyard, cursing, blaspheming, squabbling among the graves, and tearing down parts of the precincts that obstructed their play. The state outlawed it repeatedly, though always leaving loopholes for the monarch and his friends. In 1409, Henry IV ordained that all servants and labourers must 'utterly leave playing at the Balls, as well Hand-ball as Foot-ball', with a penalty of 'Imprisonment by Six Days' for infringement. Henry VIII maintained in an Act of 1511 that 'Teynes Play . . . and other unlawfull games', though repeatedly banned by 'many good and beneficiall estatutes', were behind most of the evils of the day: 'grete impoverisshement', 'many heynous Murdurs', and the fact that the safety of the realm had become imperilled because no one practised archery any more. Naturally, Henry exempted himself, commissioning his own dedicated tennis facility at Hampton Court Palace.

In the sport's heyday, which spanned roughly the early modern period, tennis fever swept across almost all major European cities and university towns. In Paris, you could hardly move for courts – a Venetian ambassador once estimated that there were 1,800 of them, though the real number was likely in the hundreds. There were courts in The Hague, in Prague, in Vienna, and in St Petersburg. In Edinburgh, between the early sixteenth and late seventeenth centuries, there were seventeen, including one at Holyrood Palace. In the eighteenth century, a court was built at the British garrison in Gibraltar for the bored officers, along with a library and billiard room. The sport generated a luxury market for clothing and equipment. In 1643, at the height of the Civil War, Charles I, hiding out in Oxford, ordered his Master of the Robes to bring him an extravagant new taffeta suit from enemy-occupied London. Balls were valued according to the material they were stuffed with. In *Sudden Death* (2013), Álvaro Enrigue's novel about a violent sixteenth-century tennis match, Anne Boleyn's executioner, a keen *jeu de paume* player, requests the queen's red braids as his fee. The 'hair of those executed on the scaffold', he knows, will 'trade at stratospheric prices among ball makers in Paris', Anne's most of all.

Money was integral to the game from the medieval period onwards. One of the earliest pictures we have of a racket, the frontispiece to a 1511 French poem, is also a picture of money. The engraving shows a male corpse stretched out on his tomb, his soul poised to be snatched by the devil. Tightly clasped under his right arm, as though he can't let go of it, is a gut-strung racket; in his left hand is a bag of gold. Like dice or cards, tennis was a game you bet on. Spectators gambled, heckling from their seats in the galleries under the penthouse after staking their cash on one side or the other. Players gambled on themselves, agreeing with one another beforehand how 'expensive' their match was going to be and stashing funds under the net. Huge sums were routinely won and lost. Henry VII's account books are a melancholy record of what it was like to be a mediocre player: 'July 5. To a new pleyer at tenes, £4.' 'For the Kinges losse at the paune [sic] pley 7s. 8d.' The 3rd Viscount Campden, MP for Rutland during the seventeenth century, received a wedding gift of £3,000 from Charles I in 1632 and promptly lost £2,500 of it at tennis in a day.

One of the most extraordinary facts about the game is that its scoring system – later taken over by lawn tennis (love, fifteen, thirty, forty) – is a vestige of this gambling culture. 'Fifteen' is thought to refer to the *gros denier tournois*, a medieval French coin worth fifteen *deniers* (pence), which was the smallest unit used to bet with. Four of these coins, amounting to sixty *deniers*, represented the maximum allowable stake and so demarcated a game. 'Love', the word for zero, seems to have derived from an old Dutch word for 'honour', *lof*. Players who failed to score any points and so win any money were described – presumably mockingly – as playing simply for the honour of taking part, the dignity of the game. To play for *lof* was to come home with zero.

Money continues to be a powerful presence in the game. After a period of decline, tennis re-emerged in Britain in the 1820s as a favourite pastime of the upper classes. New private courts began to be built on the estates of the nobility – at Stratfield Saye, the residence of the dukes of Wellington; at Hatfield House and Petworth House – and by the wealthy and lesser-titled at their country houses. In London, exclusive clubs sprang up in Mayfair, Kensington, Barons Court, and St John's Wood. When tennis was reintroduced to the US in the 1870s (a proclamation from 1659, prohibiting it during an upcoming religious day, suggests it was played in colonial New York), it was a symbol of Gilded Age affluence. The Whitney family built courts in Manhasset, Long Island, and Aiken, South Carolina. The Goulds, who made their millions on the railroads, built one in Lakewood, New Jersey. You could play tennis in downtown Boston, in the yachting paradise of Newport, Rhode Island, and in a Venetian-style palazzo on Park Avenue. (The Park Avenue Racquet & Tennis Club is now the only real tennis club in the world not to permit women members. A few years ago, through gritted teeth, I allowed my husband to play there on the condition that he perform a small act of sabotage. Gingerly, he nudged a painting askew.)

In the early modern period, at the height of its popularity, tennis was a language. Its metaphors and images were widely used by writers and artists because just about everyone had some notion of how the game worked: it allowed individuals to imagine abstract things in a shared way. In *An Essay Concerning Human Understanding* (1690), John Locke illustrated the connection between volition and liberty with reference to a well-known object: 'A tennis-ball, whether in motion by the stroke of a racket, or lying still at rest, is not by any one taken to be a free agent . . . We conceive not a tennis-ball to think, and consequently not to have any volition.' Less successfully, a fifteenth-century Dutch theologian counselled trying to understand Christ's sacrificial body on the cross as a ball cut to pieces, its red cow-hair stuffing bleeding through the leather.

Languages operate by fixed rules, which govern usage and allow us to be intelligible to one another. In sports, rules define playability. Rules are what make it possible to agree on whether a ball is in or out; whether a manoeuvre is legitimate or illegitimate; the point at which someone wins and someone loses. One of the attractions of real tennis, at least for me, is the thorniness of its rule book. Chases of 'hazard worse than the door' and 'more than a yard worse than the last gallery' make perfect sense within the context of the game. At Hatfield House Tennis Club, there is a small patch of netting, high up on the wall at the receiving end, which looks like it should be out of bounds but isn't. Hitting it is known as 'going between the goalposts': it regularly foxes visiting players. An extraordinary rule known as the 'bisque', rarely brought out nowadays, grants players one free point each per match to use whenever they wish. 'Bisque!' you might shout frantically, if you were trailing 5–4 in the final set and your opponent just served an ace. The ace would be 'undone' and you would take the point instead.

Formal aspects of real tennis are adhered to tenaciously: the predominantly white dress code; the etiquette of who passes whom at the net-post during a change of ends. These rituals shape the game's identity and distinguish it from its modern offshoots. But inflexibility can make sports seem outdated, detached from the times. At Wimbledon in 2010, John Isner and Nicolas Mahut played a 138-game final set because neither could break the other's serve. In 2019, the Championships instituted a ten-point tiebreak at twelve games all in the final set, adjusting its rules to respond to developments in playing style. Real tennis is the kind of sport that adjusts slowly, but in one area it is moving fast. Next year, in 2025, the women's World Championships will adopt a 'challenger' format for the first time: a handful of the top players will compete for the right to challenge the current world champion. The hope is that introducing an arrangement similar to that of the men's World Championships will elevate the women's game, producing more competitive, elite-level matches. The old 'sport of kings' is flexing, expanding gently at the seams. ∎

EVENTS ASHORE

An-My Lê

Introduction by Granta

For nine years, the photographer An-My Lê tracked her prey: the United States military. Designed to face down conventional enemies, it hasn't won a war since 1991. Still, it remains the most visually impressive fighting force in the world.

Lê's photographs possess a disarming lucidity, but with a twist that makes peculiar demands on the viewer. Her images from *Events Ashore* allow the pristine idealism of the military recruits to sit alongside the acknowledgment of the extraordinary violence her subjects have been trained to inflict.

A caste apart from American society, the US military has different codes, different discipline and a different economic system. Lê serenely documents how it thrusts its way into every part of the globe. She captures soldiers as they disembark at ports, polish fighter jets, provide earthquake relief, lounge in bars, and embed in lush landscapes.

The sunbathers on the beach here could be sybarites from a Patricia Highsmith novel, until we look closer. The opening photograph of the sailor seems like a standard fulfillment of duty, though undercut by the knowledge that there are the likes of Chelsea Manning and Aaron Bushnell among the rank and file. ∎

Forward Look Out,
USS Tortuga, Gulf
of Thailand, 2010

Platoon Marine
Corps Expeditionary
Unit, Shoalwater Bay,
Australia, 2007

EA-6B Prowler Engines Ready for Firing Up, USS Ronald Reagan, North Arabian Gulf, 2009

USS Nashville, Dakar, Senegal, 2009

American Sailors Returning to Vietnam, First U.S. Naval Exchange Activities with Vietnam People's Navy, Da Nang, Vietnam, 2009

Visit, Board, Search, and Seizure Operations Demonstration for Mauritius Police Force, USS Arleigh Burke, 2009

Indonesian Marines with
U.S. Army Interpreter,
Pohakuloa Training
Area, Hawaii, 2012

Marine Corps Weapons Company (I), Earthquake Relief, Grand Goave, Haiti, 2010

Assault of a Fortified
Position Supported,
Princess Patricia's
Canadian Light Infantry,
Pohakuloa Training
Area, Hawaii, 2012

Swedish Ice Breakers
Oden, McMurdo
Sound, Antarctica,
2008

Landing Signal
officers, USS Ronald
Reagan, North
Arabian Gulf, 2009

Seabees on Liberty,
Naval Mobile
Construction Battalion,
Moroni Beach,
Comoros, 2009

Boatswain's Mate
Driving at the Helm,
USS Nashville,
Atlantic Ocean, 2009

Conning Officer and
Ensign Navigating
USS Nashville,
Atlantic Ocean, 2009

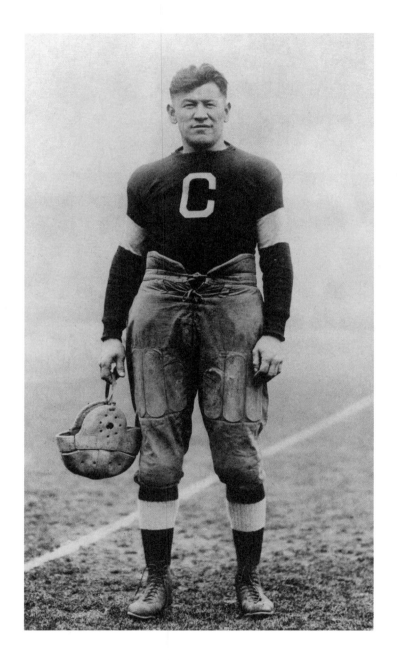

Jim Thorpe playing for the Canton Bulldogs
1915–1920

MUCKER PLAY

Nico Walker

'That's the week I scored a touchdown for the Falcons
and hit a home run for the Yankees, so that was a
special time for me, too.'

– Deion Sanders, *Power, Money, & Sex: How Success
Almost Ruined My Life*

1

American football was never invented; it was fashioned by
committee, over a span of decades. The first college All-
Americans list went to press in 1889, seventeen years before the
game's adoption of the forward pass, thirty-eight years before the first
recorded sighting of the ball now claimed as its namesake. 1905 was
a catalyst year, the year the sitting president of the United States got
involved. Teddy Roosevelt counted himself an advocate for the sport,
professing the belief that the game's inherent violence was wholesome
for the character of American boys. When he spoke on the subject
he made vague and ominous references to future difficulties, saying
the boys would need to be tough for the times to come. Yet it had
been brought to his attention that the sport was infected with an
ungentlemanly virus, that cheaters and hoodlums plagued collegiate

football, and that schoolboys were being coached in the art of 'mucker play' – the deliberate injuring of an opponent in order to remove him from the game.

There were reasons for concern. In the wanton day of mass-formation play, of the Princeton V and the flying wedge, football was averaging about fourteen players killed per annum. Chancellors, athletic directors, and boards of overseers were under pressure to ban the sport. Roosevelt wanted to avoid that outcome. Three universities controlled the rules committee of the Intercollegiate Football Association (IFA): Harvard, Princeton, and Yale, and so Roosevelt summoned representatives from all three to meet with him at the White House on 9 October 1905. Football was on trial, said Roosevelt. To save the game, the IFA would need to reform it. There was only the matter of how.

The forward pass was suggested. At the time, a player could throw the ball backwards or laterally but not upfield. The team on defense could commit all its players to attacking the offense's backfield, and the offense didn't have much chance outside of out-bludgeoning the defense. Scoring was rare and far from assured. Apart from the violence, the games were uneventful slogs, melees, devoid of finesse. Some hoped a forward pass would change things – players would be more spread out; the game better balanced, safer, more dynamic. With more field to take into account, teams would not concentrate into mass formations, and defenses would have to commit players to guard the area behind their lines.

The Yale contingent balked at the idea. They suspected Roosevelt had an ulterior motive: helping his alma mater Harvard (their arch rival) gain an advantage over them. Representing Yale was Walter Camp, the (unofficial) director of its football team. Camp was no lightweight: the line of scrimmage; the eleven men on a side (down from fifteen); the safety penalty and it being worth two points; the point system itself – all these and more were his contributions to the genesis of the game. He had been in attendance at the 1873 meeting when the IFA was formed; his name was on the rule book; in 1892

Harper's Weekly had called him 'the father of American football'. It would be a great help for Roosevelt's reform initiative if he could talk Camp into throwing his support behind it.

This seemed within the realm of possibility. Camp's crowning achievement, the line of scrimmage, had been a player-safety measure. When he took it to the Rules Committee, he brought statistics that showed the greatest number of injuries happened in scrums. If Camp had been for improving player safety then, it stood to reason he could be coaxed to be so again. But the forward pass was anathema to Camp, for whom the essence of the sport was the ground attack. In his game, an edge was sought by forming as many of your players into as fine a point as possible and running it through the adversarial body. Football strategists of the day thought in terms of phalanxes and legions, studied battle formations back to ancient Macedonia in search of an insight, some irresistible spearhead lost to time.

However much Roosevelt dug him, Camp wasn't won over. He wasn't some uneducated sucker – he was a Yale man, a member of Skull and Bones, and the top power broker in football, a schemer with a $100,000 slush fund who for decades had been calling the shots for the Eli of Yale from his office at the New Haven Clock Company. The White House meeting adjourned with no promise from Camp beyond a commitment to join the others in issuing a public condemnation of mucker play, and a pledge to clean up the game from any disgraceful, unsportsmanlike or immoral element.

Roosevelt was quick to declare victory. In a letter to Camp, he expressed effusive satisfaction, writing of his trust in the integrity of the football men and in their ability to enact reforms that would restore the game to good standing. Seven weeks later, three players were killed, all on one Saturday, 25 November 1905. The names of the dead ran in the *Chicago Tribune*: 'Those Killed Yesterday . . . OSBORN, CARL, 18 years old, Marshall, Ind.: killed in game of Judson high school vs. Bellmore high school; injured in tackle, rib piercing heart and killing him almost instantly . . . MOORE, WILLIAM, right half back of Union college; killed in game with New

York university; fractured skull in bucking the line: died in hospital . . . Fatally Injured . . . BROWN, ROBERT, 15 years old, Sedalia, Mo.; paralyzed from neck down; dying.' The headline read: FOOTBALL YEAR'S DEATH HARVEST: RECORDS SHOW THAT NINETEEN PLAYERS HAVE BEEN KILLED; ONE HUNDRED THIRTY-SEVEN HURT.

Over that Thanksgiving break, Columbia, Duke, and Northwestern universities went ahead and banned football, having lost patience with the Rules Committee. Predictably, Roosevelt was outraged and vowed action. Using his executive powers as commander-in-chief of the United States Armed Forces, he ordered the military academies to come to their own consensus on a new set of rules. He wasn't the only one making moves. Chancellor of New York University Henry MacCracken and Harvard coach Bill Reid were arranging an emergency meeting of sixty-two colleges and universities. The newly assembled body called itself the Intercollegiate Athletic Association of the United States. Its first order of business was to take a vote on whether or not to ban football. A general ban fell short by two votes. The next step was to revise the rules. Camp had been usurped – not being present he was unable to argue for the sanctity of the ground attack. Legalization of the forward pass was a foregone conclusion.

The first legal forward pass was attempted on the first weekend of the 1906 season. Bradbury Robinson of St Louis University tried it out against Carroll College. The pass fell incomplete, which made the play illegal. In the 1906 rules, a forward pass was legal only if completed – an incomplete pass was a penalty, and the penalty was a turnover, which meant the passing team lost possession of the ball. Here was the problem: the forward pass had only been legalized by half measures, relegated to the status of a trick play, a play you ought to be embarrassed to try, that you should be penalized for if unsuccessful. You could try to shoot the devil in the back, but if you missed then the devil got the ball and, in the name of the father of American football, God willing, rammed it down your throat, ground-and-pound style. There was still no penalty for pass interference, which meant the defense was at liberty to tackle the receiver mid-route. Anybody stout enough to run a pass route and not get knocked down was unlikely to have enough speed to get open and vice versa. Most teams stuck to the ground game.

Camp continued politicking for the repeal of the forward pass, on the grounds it left the outcome of games too much to chance, that an undeserving team might win. His time dictating the precepts of the sport meant that he still held sway over football men throughout the country, and many were not quick to relinquish the philosophy they had imbibed from him. But the problem for opponents to the forward pass was that players kept dying. The 1909 season saw twenty-six players killed in action. As had been going on for thirty years, most of the dead were high-school players – to put it another way, children – and less and less did people care what the Father of American Football was saying about the essence of the game.

The 1910 season was inaugurated with the forward pass on equal legal footing as run plays. The new era could now begin in earnest. Purists of the day said American football was ruined forever.

2

O ut of these ruins green shoots did grow, and a new game flowered and spread. The forward pass proved to be an equalizer. Before the forward pass, whoever could acquire the most body, the most beef, was the favorite to win. Now speed, agility, timing, and field vision counted almost as much as pure violence. Glenn Scobey 'Pop' Warner perceived these things, since he had an interest in working them to his advantage. When he first arrived at the Carlisle Indian Industrial School in Carlisle, Pennsylvania, to take over the job as head coach of the Carlisle Indians, the team had already competed against top schools and held their own well enough. But Carlisle's teams tended to be underweight, shorter in height and reach than their competition. To overcome this they outmaneuvered, out-schemed, and out-executed their opponents. Warner was an established journeyman coach, with a reputation for running up the score on the other team. He was ready for the forward pass. In 1911, Warner and Carlisle went 11–1.

The next year, the Carlisle team won its most poetic victory: 9 November 1912, Carlisle Indian Industrial School versus Army at West Point. Three thousand were in attendance, and the symbolism not lost on one of them. Warner professed himself not one for pregame speeches, but in this case he made an exception: 'I shouldn't have to prepare you for this game, just go read your history books. Remember that it was the fathers and grandfathers of these Army players who fought your fathers and grandfathers in the Indian Wars. Remember it was their fathers and grandfathers who killed your fathers and grandfathers. Remember this, every play. These men playing against you are the soldiers. They are the Long Knives. You are Indians. Tonight, we will know if you are warriors.'

The game was remembered for its roughness. Carlisle got off to a shaky start, shut out for most of the first half by a score of 6–0. The second half was another story. Warner's star tailback Jim Thorpe ran riot. The Army team went to pieces. The Cadets targeted Thorpe. Mucker play. But Thorpe was 'impervious to injury', and the attention Army paid him freed up Alex Arcasa at halfback to score three touchdowns. Army kept trying to move the ball on offense and showed a spark of life when freshman halfback Dwight 'the Kansas Cyclone' Eisenhower ripped off a twelve-yard run almost to midfield, not quite into Carlisle territory. Eisenhower tried to knock Thorpe out of the game, went for him so hard he missed the mark when Thorpe juked him and crashed into the Army halfback Leland Hobbs instead. Hobbs had to be carried off the field. Eisenhower sat out the rest of the game with a knee injury – the Kansas Cyclone would never play again. Carlisle didn't let off after that. The game was called a few minutes early due to a lack of light. Carlisle beat Army 27–6.

The Army team captain, first-team All-American tackle Leland Devore had been disqualified for unnecessary roughness. Devore would go on to take part in Black Jack Pershing's 'Punitive Expedition' against Mexico in 1916, and then to serve as an infantry officer in France, where he would be wounded, one of several American football standouts to be injured in the Great War. The linebacker, Eisenhower, missed that one; perhaps his knee kept him out or perhaps he was just lucky. The Second World War he wasn't as lucky. The Army put him in charge of Overlord; he was smoking five packs of cigarettes a day; he had an affair with his secretary; he tried to resign; the Chief of Staff laughed in his face, told him to get real, told him to mash the button. And he did the deed. Americans were so grateful they elected him president, and they liked the job he did so much they elected him again. At the end of his second term, in a speech to the Republican National Committee, his thoughts wandered to his counterpart from the Carlisle–Army game of 1912: 'Here and there, there are some people who are supremely endowed. My memory goes back to Jim Thorpe. He never practiced in his life, and he could do anything better than any other football player I ever saw.'

Such was the stature and reputation of Wa-Tho-Huk (Bright Path), government name James Francis Thorpe, of the Sac and Fox Nation. Jim Thorpe became the greatest football player of all time. He was among the first players for the National Football League, a new professional league founded in 1920 – now the highest-grossing league in American sport.

Thorpe went on to fame and glory – Pop Warner to a season of infamy. He was discovered by the Department of Interior to be in league with Carlisle superintendent Moses Friedman playing fast and loose with the money. Carlisle was foul to begin with, the school being an instrument of genocide. The students, young Native American men and women, were taught that their cultures were inferior to European culture, forced to disown their customs and rituals and to attend Christian religious services. The food was rough, the discipline strict, the books cooked. Of the over 10,000 youths to attend Carlisle since its founding, hundreds had died and many were buried there, far from home, under names that were not their own.

The public image of Pop Warner, surrogate father, leader of men, benevolent genius, progressive white man: it was exposed as a fake. The players knew who Warner was. They knew he was getting rich off of them or else he wouldn't have been there in the first place. Perhaps the most striking example was the presence of Warner in hotel lobbies selling the comp tickets the home team gave the Carlisle team when they came to town to play. One Carlisle football player testified that he saw Warner sell seventy-five such tickets on one occasion, seventy-five being the total number of tickets the home team had set aside for the visitors. The player said he never found out what Warner did with that money. The Carlisle Indian Industrial School was closed down in 1918. Taken over by the Department of the Army, it was converted to Base Hospital 31. Carlisle was forgotten. Army had its revenge.

3

And so they broke the mold when they made Jim Thorpe. He was the first football player of international fame. At the 1912 Olympics in Stockholm, Thorpe won gold twice, for the penthalon and the decathalon, and the King of the Swedes, Gustav V, declared him 'the greatest athlete in the world'. To have have an athlete of Thorpe's stature suiting up for games was a windfall of legitimacy for the sport.

Thorpe was the model figure that would define American football for a generation: the star tailback. See, the quarterback, the present day's most exalted position in the sport, he wasn't drawing much attention in those days. The QB's role was more as a blocker. Even with the advent of the forward pass, the QB's physical interaction with the football was largely limited to receiving it from the center and giving it away as quickly as he could. The center would 'snap' the ball – originally, by rolling it backwards with his heel; later on, by passing it back through his legs into the hands of the QB – and the next move would usually be for the QB to toss pitch or shovel pass the ball back to a teammate deeper in the offense's backfield, getting the ball away from the opponent's defensive line as it tried to crash in. The QB could not legally advance the ball forward of the line of scrimmage before moving laterally five yards to either side of the spot the center had snapped the ball from.

The one privilege of being quarterback was that, as the conduit of the ball to the playmakers in the backfield, it was a leadership position. It was the quarterback's job to manage the game, to see who on his team was hot, to see where the defense was weak and make adjustments, call the right play. The quarterback did the snap count. The quarterback held the ball for the kicker on placekicks. The quarterback was an indispensable ball-handler, much as he is now.

But there was a stretch of roughly thirty years – from the 1920s through the 1940s – when the quarterback wasn't getting a lot of touches. He called the plays and the signals, he blocked, maybe caught a few passes, he held kicks. But he hardly did any passing. The tailback was the focus of the offense, the feature back. Not only could he be the primary rusher, he could be the primary passer, too. And so for a while the sport revolved around the tailback, and the dominant tailbacks were easy to make famous. Thorpe played in the single-wing scheme, as designed by Warner. The tailback and the fullback started five yards deep in the backfield, on either side of the center, so that the center had the option of snapping the ball to either of them. The QB would be lined up behind the tackle. A wingback, the namesake of the formation, would set up off the back foot of one of the ends. The QB and the wingback could block, or they could break upfield and look for a pass. The games tended to be open, with lateral running. The tailback had to go five yards to a side of the snapper before he could turn upfield, the backs would run a sweep, the three backs lead-blocking for the tailback. It was vital to beat the defense to the corner. The runner had to turn the corner and break into the defensive backfield to get free.

To have a track star like Thorpe, a player with that kind of speed, was a decisive advantage. The opponent's defense had to work hard to have a chance to stop the run, and yet it could not fully commit so long as the offense had the option of throwing a forward pass. The wingback could always throw a block first, say, on a sweep, and then dump the defender and break off into a pass route upfield. The threat kept defenses off balance. The game was becoming more tactically complex. And Thorpe was up for that. He could kick the ball better than anybody. He could throw the ball well, as he had thrown the discus well, and the shot put. His prowess was the means by which the game's next phase was demonstrated.

The game had now begun to resemble its current form. There were still many limitations in place to hamper the passing game. Since 1906 the field had been marked into grids, five-by-five yards, and a forward pass couldn't cross the line of scrimmage in the same grid as the ball was snapped in. The turf conditions were generally bad. Games played in the rain would devolve into a mostly inert brawl, purchase could not be gained for love or money, the teams wallowing in muck. The thirty-yard reception wasn't yet visible on the horizon. Again, the football – the actual ball itself – still hadn't been invented. The sport was played with a rugby ball, no matter what anybody says, which was more difficult to throw – particularly, to spiral – so there were lobs or there were forward laterals, a bit of razzle-dazzle, like a game of keep-away, one that looked at home on silent-movie reels, maybe with some stride piano to accompany it, or a slide trombone.

For all its grasping awkwardness, as the sport struggled to loose itself from the primordial mud of its creation, it photographed well. The chaotic brawl, when distilled into a single photographic frame, assumed a gravitas that not even the live action itself could match. The football player became more than just a chauvinist preppy who liked to hurt people. Thorpe marked the point in time when the football player began to symbolize something higher than a game. Regardless of how he felt about it, a myth was constructed around him.

As it often did then and would continue to do, baseball helped football along. Thorpe had played baseball well enough at Carlisle to be considered a viable big-league talent, and the National League's New York Giants (of baseball) were eager to sign him. They knew

Thorpe's celebrity would sell tickets, at least for a while, perhaps for a long time, should it turn out he could play. In 1913, the Giants signed Thorpe to a $6,000-a-year contract, a record payout for a rookie at that time. He didn't play very well. It could've been he struggled to bat at a big-league level. It was rumored he couldn't hit the curveball. It was rumored Giants manager John McGraw had spread that rumor.

In the 1951 motion picture *Jim Thorpe – All-American*, Thorpe's failure to make good in Major League Baseball is blamed on a lack of discipline and an incurable stubbornness of character. In the scene that's supposed to demonstrate this, the actor who plays McGraw fines Burt Lancaster (as Thorpe) $50 for ignoring a signal to bunt. 'I got a hit, didn't I?' says Lancaster. 'That's not the point,' the actor playing McGraw says, 'this is a team game.' What the film fails to mention was that if this exchange had in fact happened, then there would've likely been a piece of rope in McGraw's possession at the time – a 'good luck charm' he carried with him – which had been used in the lynching of a Black man, because McGraw was one of the monumental racists of baseball history. Which is all to say that Thorpe's difficulties could've been down to McGraw's Giants not being the ideal team for Jim Thorpe.

Or it could be that Jim Thorpe was never that interested in playing baseball. He showed up, and he sold the tickets. He hacked away. But what was there for Jim Thorpe to love in the game of baseball? He wasn't the pitcher on the mound. The game's outcome wasn't entirely riding upon his shoulders. Consequently he must have felt frustrated, squandered, too talented for his role on that team.

In gridiron football, not only did the outcome of any given game depend on him, the survival of the league he played for depended on him. The Olympics had made him into a celebrity, yet at the same time baseball was baseball, the 'American Pastime', and to have a high-profile major-leaguer like Thorpe split his time between the premier sport in American culture and football was a life-sustaining elevation for the new professional teams. Thorpe was making $250 a game, setting a new high for what qualified as top dollar in football.

He played for the Bulldogs of Canton, Ohio. He was also head coach. Before signing Thorpe, the Bulldogs' attendance receipts were averaging around 1,500 spectators. Thorpe's debut saw attendance jump to 8,000. He stayed with the team from 1915 through 1920, the last being the year a new pro league was founded in Canton, the American Professional Football Association, which, two years later, was renamed the National Football League.

4

In the US presidential race of 1916 the incumbent candidate, diehard Princeton football fan Woodrow Wilson, ran on the slogan 'He kept us out of war', and he got re-elected like that, knowing full well he was going to take the country to war immediately, wasn't even going to wait until after the midterms. Since there was going to be a draft, there'd need to be a fitness regimen, something to whip the boys into shape. President Wilson tapped Camp to come up with something. Camp came up with the daily dozen, twelve exercises which, if done regularly, could transform a young man's physique, change him from a fledgling into a man who could kill you with just his bare hands. Football was part of the program. At the forts, camps, and bases throughout the country, recruits from all over were playing American football. When the war ended and the boys came home, they came home knowing a lot more about football than they did when they left. It was the beginning of a long and beautiful relationship, the triad of American football, the American war machine, and the American male.

There'd be more room yet for American football on the national stage, and room too for football stars, tailbacks like Jim Thorpe, only different. In the 1920s there was Red Grange. Born Harold Grange, he developed a knack for nicknames early. Harry Grange wasn't going to get his name in the papers, so he became Red Grange, then when he was a high-school standout he became the Iceman of Wheaton, because he worked part-time as a deliverer on an ice truck. Then he went to play for Illinois, the Fighting Illini. He came into the game in a fog, looking like a ghost, and the ghost could run the ball, and so they called him the Galloping Ghost. He could run, he could throw, and like Thorpe he went pro. He left school early, the star tailback cutting out on his team. But Red was right: why kill yourself for the school colors when you could be making a killing on the free market playing for the Chicago Bears in the NFL? The newspapers howled about it, the old boys dog cursed him, but the public didn't care. The public didn't go to college.

Like Thorpe, Grange legitimized the professional leagues. The best football player in the country ditched school to wear a fur coat and drive a Cadillac. What wasn't there to love about that? This was the democratization of the football star. It wasn't esoteric East Coast college-boy role-play anymore. It was something the man in the street could get behind. It reminded him of war in ways that were good. It made him feel tough to know that there were tough men making money playing ball and eating steaks two inches thick. It gave him something to dream about. It was upward mobility embodied, the tailback running into the pile, shedding tacklers, breaking into the open field, running bastards over, free now, running free into the end zone, still running all the way through the tunnel, out of the stadium, into the limousine, to the best table and the best club in town, dinner and a few drinks, see everybody, and then home to the big house on the hill.

Red Grange could be you. Red Grange, the boy who'd been born in the logging camps of Forksville, PA, the boy whose mother died and whose daddy went home to Wheaton, IL, and got a job as a policeman. Red Grange, just a regular guy. If you weren't Jim Thorpe, you could be Red Grange. In the 1930s you could be the Four Horsemen of Notre Dame. Improvements in motion-picture technology helped to get the word out, and with the pads on the boys looked impressive. The headgear reminded people of aviators. If you were trying to sell a few newspapers, you couldn't hurt your cause by bringing God into it, at least when His team was doing good. This proliferation of publicity would have a lasting impact. Had it not been for the Four Horsemen of Notre Dame, a Catholic like John F. Kennedy probably couldn't have been elected in the 1960 presidential election. Kennedy was standing on the shoulders of giants, four football players who had put in the work in South Bend, Indiana, and endeared papism to even the most jingo-Protestant hearts.

Then came the aptly named Bronko Nagurski. Like Grange, Bronko played for the Bears. They were teammates from 1930 to 1934; Grange at tailback in the sunset of his playing career, Bronko at fullback, just at his outset. They inadvertently ended the tailback era of football together, in a game in 1932. Nagurski faked a run, dropped back and threw a touchdown pass to Grange. It was the NFL's first ever playoff game, the Chicago Bears versus the Portsmouth Spartans. The game had been moved indoors at the last minute due to a snowstorm, and so the referees didn't have the benefit of the grid to keep players (like Nagurski) honest. The Spartans complained to the league officials on hand, saying that the play had been illegal, that Nagurski clearly had been closer than five yards to the line of scrimmage when he'd thrown the pass. The points had to be taken away, they said. The league's answer was to change the rule. The grid went out the window, replaced by the hash-mark system that's used to mark the playing field today. It was the beginning of the modern era, part of which would entail player specialties – e.g. a separation of powers between the feature running back and the passer; between the fullback and the kicker, etc.

Bronko and Grange were the last of their generation. Never again would an offense's plans rely so much on the effort of one player, a combination of the modern game's running back and quarterback and kicker in one position. There would be no more iron men like that, a back that could carry the whole team on his shoulders, run the ball, score all the touchdowns, pass upfield, kick a field goal, go out for a pass just to mix things up, do a little upfield blocking – and in the days of the one platoon system, when teams didn't rotate players when they went from offense to defense, the eleven players who started the game meant to play every down. The game was a struggle of violent endurance. The players were workhorses, and they played through injury. They didn't want to lose their jobs. It was a perfect allegory for the times.

Who was this tailback? This Achilles? Was he John Henry? Was he a try-hard? A fat cat? A warrior prince? A scab? Did it matter who won? Why did these men, these guards and tackles and ends and centers – men who weren't getting paid like the stars in the backfield were getting paid – why did they go out and break their neck for the tailback so he could score his touchdown, so the coach could win, so the owner could win, so the city could win, so the fans could be happy? Because it was beautiful to see. Bronko, the ultimate expression of an era of the running back, tearing into the wind on a frozen field, north Chicago, Wrigley Field, the wind coming in off the cold lake, wind that could freeze a man to death, but not Bronko. Bronko liked to go to war like that, busting linebackers in the chops, went to war for his team, for his buddies, for his people – the Polacks, in this case.

Bronko played until 1937. Everybody knew he was going to be the last star of his kind. The rules had changed and teams needed to adapt to new kinds of offense, or they would lose. It was the end of the grid game. It was the professional sport wresting control of the game from the collegiate leagues. The team owners didn't have universities backing them, they had to make money, and they figured it'd be nice to see more scoring.

So the NFL introduced the modern ball. The 1934 ball was modified from the more rugby-esque style of ball; the altered version had tapered ends, making the ball easier to grip and, therefore, easier to throw a spiral. It must have seemed as though the forward pass were being invented all over again. The game changed suddenly and profoundly. In the 1934 season, the leading passer in the NFL was Arnie 'Flash' Herber, who threw for 799 yards (that's passing yards gained from scrimmage). In 1937, 'Slingin' Sammy' Baugh threw for 1,127. In 1945, Sid Luckman threw for 1,727 yards. In 1955, Jimmy Finks threw for 2,270.

Bronko Nagurski, 1929
Chicago History Museum

The quarterback knew what everybody's role in every play was –
who should zig, who should zag. So the quarterback was the natural
choice to be the offense's dedicated passer, provided he could throw
– like *really* throw. If he couldn't *really* throw, he wasn't going to play
quarterback anymore.

The QB got billed as the star of the show. All that was missing
was television. It wasn't long in coming, almost as though it had
been waiting. 28 December 1958 saw the first broadcast of the NFL
Championship Game between the Indianapolis Colts and the New
York Giants. The Colts won in sudden-death overtime. Forty-five
million people were said to have watched the game, and afterwards
American football was made. No power on Earth could stop it from

becoming the most popular sport in the country, because the future of sports was on television, and football seemed made for TV. The TV would never do justice to the fastball or the curveball. The baseball field was too big to fit on the screen, you were looking one way, then another way, or you were looking one way, then this way, or you were looking from so far back you couldn't see anything. The TV was better suited to spectacular violence – football.

It helped that the football schedules formatted so well to network programming; a reasonable number of games that did not take up too much airtime, yet filled enough of it every year so as to be indispensable. Baseball teams played 154 games a year. That was a lot of TV time to spend on keeping up with a single team. NFL teams only played thirteen games a year, not counting the playoffs. College teams played ten, eleven games. The colleges played Saturday, the pros Sunday. You could theoretically follow two football teams closely and still hold on to your job. This was now the American century, and the war machine was always in the wings.

War was embedded deep into the sport, everywhere in the vernacular. The sack. The wedge. The line. The blitz. In its infancy, football had reveled in its homage to pre-gunpowder war, to melee combat. The tailback era alluded to war on horseback, to the cavalry. The Galloping Ghost. The Four Horsemen. The modern game, the quarterback game, looked for its reflection in aerial warfare. Receivers ran 'routes' or 'patterns'. Teams had their offensive and defensive schemes. There was the 'long bomb'. Bobby Layne was 'the Blond Bomber', Daryle Lamonica was 'the Mad Bomber'. Footage of teams studying plays on the board, the players sitting at little desks in a classroom, brought to mind bomber pilots being briefed by their commanders with maps and aerial photographs of targets. It all made for compelling television. America was strong, and so was American football. It was on Sunday, just like church. It was a religious service now. The religion was America. And America was the business of war. It seemed like it could go on forever.

5

I t was no coincidence that the quarterback always used to be a white guy. The same year the so-called modern era of American football began, 1933, was the same year the NFL locked in its period of infamy, the era of the 'gentlemen's agreement' – the unspoken pact between NFL owners not to sign Black players to contracts. College football had never barred Black players from playing because it didn't have to. How many Black men were admitted to Princeton or Harvard or Yale or Columbia? There were a few Black players: William Henry Lewis played for Harvard, William Tecumseh Sherman Jackson for Amherst, George Jewett for the University of Michigan. Paul Robeson played for Rutgers. It wasn't until the sport got big that the bigots began to take notice of who was playing in the games.

The bosses were putting the screws down everywhere. Fascism was on the rise, at home and abroad. The police were for sale. The means of production were not up for discussion. George Preston Marshall, owner of the Boston Braves, was intending to move the team to Washington, D.C. In 1933, Washington, D.C. was a segregated city, as it would be up until 1953. And the owners were worried a race riot would break out if Black players were getting paid while white men were out of work.

Segregation stuck for twelve years. In that time there was another world war. The second. Another Roosevelt was president. Franklin Delano. Traitor to his class, they said. He sent his segregated armies of democracy to fight overseas. Twenty-one NFL players were killed. The rest were in pieces, shot up or shell-shocked, missing toes, doing morphine, committing suicide, working for General Motors.

Segregation made American football meaningless: it kept the best players from playing. In 1946, the NFL was officially reintegrated. But it is difficult to place an exact date on when the NFL was actually desegregated, because internal segregation persisted. Black players were shut out of leadership positions: quarterback, middle linebacker. The hostility ended up backfiring on the bigots. In order for a Black

Jim Brown of the Cleveland Browns on a Topps
football trading card, 1959

man to make it onto the football field, he had to be multiples better
than his white counterparts. And when it happened, people noticed.

For example, Jim Brown. He ran the ball and kicked field goals for
the Syracuse Orangemen and would've won the Heisman Trophy,
had the Heisman Committee given it to the best football player that
year, and not the best white football player. But he had his revenge
when he turned pro in 1957. In his first season, he set a single-game
rushing record – 237 yards – that stood fourteen years, and a rookie
rushing record – 942 yards over twelve games – that stood forty
years. He won Rookie of the Year and his first MVP. Next he broke
the single-season rushing record, surpassing Steve Van Buren by just
short of 400 yards. The only year he didn't win the NFL rushing title
was 1962, when he was hampered by injury. There was nothing on
the field that Brown couldn't accomplish. He retired at age thirty,

having already cemented his reputation as the greatest American football player since Jim Thorpe, and while he was still in his prime.

His retirement was international news. Brown was in England, filming *The Dirty Dozen*, about a band of military prison convicts sent behind enemy lines to kill the Nazi high command at a cocktail party in occupied Normandy. In the film, Jim Brown's character Jefferson sacrifices his life to drop hand grenades through the air shafts onto the heads of Nazi partygoers cowering in a bomb shelter. There were filming delays, and the project was running behind. Brown hadn't intended to miss his team's training camp, but his hands were tied. *The Dirty Dozen* wasn't a B-picture. It had blockbuster talent: Lee Marvin, Charles Bronson, Donald Sutherland, John Cassavetes, Telly Savalas, Ernest Borgnine, George Kennedy, Trini Lopez, Robert Phillips. His team owner wasn't thinking about that. Art Modell let it be known he would fine Jim Brown for every day of training camp he missed. The message wasn't well received. Brown had been carrying Modell's team on his back, now going on nine years. He decided that he would rather retire from football than deal with it anymore. His kiss-off to the NFL made him more famous than he had ever been while playing. He retired in 1966. Twenty years after the integration of the NFL, a Black man was turning the league down.

6

The NFL didn't take the lead in integrating football. That honor belonged to another league. In the late 1950s, Lamar Hunt, heir to the Texas oil fortune of his father, the arch-conservative H.L. Hunt, was determined to buy a football team. H.L. Hunt had bestowed a trust worth more than $500 million to his son, so that Lamar could be 'self-employed' and build something of his own. But the owners of the NFL didn't want him in the club. There were stories about him, that he and his daddy were mobbed up; later there would be talk of connections in Dallas, connections in Washington, connections to gunmen, guys with names like Ruby and Oswald.

When the NFL wouldn't expand, Lamar went looking for a team that might be for sale. There were the indigent Cardinals of Chicago. The owner Walter Wolfner rejected his offer, but he told Hunt about who else had tried to buy his team and where to find them. Hunt went down the list Wolfner provided. He made a proposition to Bud Adams, another millionaire oilman's son. Hunt laid out his plan: if they both wanted to buy a team and so did some other guys, and if the American public couldn't get enough of football on TV, why couldn't a new league succeed? Denver and Minneapolis were in, but for the league to have a national image, he'd need teams in New York and LA. Barron Hilton came on board to found the LA Chargers. The team that eventually became the New York Jets was owned by Harry Wismer.

The American Football League was formed in 1960. From the beginning, the teams included Black players. It also had different rules that improved the game – e.g. the two-point conversion, an import from the collegiate game that wouldn't be included in NFL football until the 1994 season. But the real level up was the way they did TV. The new league struck a deal with ABC. They broadcast their games right after the NFL game went off on NBC. The AFL broadcast was self-evidently better than the NFL broadcast. They featured more close-ups and new mics were developed to pick up the sound of the punt. They put the players' names on the backs of the jerseys, and the broadcasts included interviews with players before and after the games. The half-time show was not infrequently a literal circus performance, with elephants marching on the field. If Hunt liked it, it was going to happen. He was the one who knew the words 'Super' and 'Bowl' belonged together. The AFL teams went aggressively after the loyalty of their locality when there was a rival outfit in town. Most of the early AFL stadiums were down at heel, but they also had fewer rules. The game was a party. Fans brought barbecues into the stands with them.

AFL viewership was helped by the NFL's blackout policy, which barred home games from being broadcast in the area where they were played. What was on TV were the AFL games. In 1961, the AFL came up with another innovation to drum up fan support: the All-Star game. The fourth AFL All-Star Game, in 1965, was to take place in New Orleans, a state that lagged behind in civil rights, evident from the moment the players arrived. They were told they'd have to arrange rides to their hotels with a 'colored cab' service. The first evening before practice the players went out in the French Quarter, and all the Black players were turned away from clubs. They skipped practice the next day to have a meeting.

The Black All-stars from both teams were adamant about a boycott. Veteran player Cookie Gilchrist, six foot two and 225 pounds, called for a vote, adding, 'You all know I will kick the ass of whoever votes to stay and play.' The result was unanimous. White players Ron Mix and Jack Kemp tried to persuade the Black players to limit their protest to making statements to the press. But they weren't playing. The players elected Ernie Ladd, the largest player among them, at six foot nine and 325 pounds, to announce the boycott. The game was duly moved to a stadium in Houston.

7

By the end of the 1950s, the success of AFL had begotten a war between the leagues. The NFL's players used this as leverage to help themselves. Until 1956, players had no benefits, and owners had free rein to do as they wished: no minimum salary, no health insurance, no pension, no life insurance, no pay for pre-season games. This all changed when the Green Bay Packers were refused clean jocks, socks, and uniforms for two-a-day workouts that summer. The Packers organized, and joined efforts already under way in Cleveland. The National Football League Players Association (NFLPA) was formed in 1956, though it was not recognized until 1958.

At the union's first official meeting, the list of requests was basic: a minimum salary at $5,000 per year, a uniform per diem for players and equipment, and, most importantly, salary for injured players.

They submitted requests and waited for a meeting with NFL owners that never came.

The AFL formed its own union in 1964, which only worked to strengthen the demands of the NFLPA: there was the expectation that players could use the threat of signing with an AFL team to have their demands met. Players wanted a pension plan, but the owners struck back, adding a clause that any player would lose his pension if he went to another league. Any remaining hope that the two unions might aid players through collective bargaining turned to dust when, in 1966, a merger between the AFL and NFL was announced. Both unions opposed the merger, citing antitrust laws, but their meager funds weren't enough to mount an effective fight against the now all-powerful combined NFL.

The merger was not officially recognized until 1970 and the two unions still operated separately for a time – a mistake, as the owners were able to play the unions against each other. They struggled to communicate with their own membership and the NFL refused to discuss their agenda. In 1970 the players went on strike, after a lockout by the owners. But the owners threatened to cancel the season, and the strike lasted only two days. An agreement was reached: modest increases in minimum salaries, with dental benefits added. For the first time, players were given the right to have agents. Biggest of all: the agreement gave players representation on the Retirement Board and more ability to fight for injury grievances.

In 1974, new negotiations began. A system had been put in place since the NFL's beginning in which players were expected to accept their pay, perform their roles, and be grateful. The NFLPA prepared to go after the so-called 'Rozelle Rule', named for NFL commissioner Pete Rozelle, who had final say over a player's worth and where they played, a power wielded to such an extent that free agency – the players' ability to freely negotiate contracts with other teams – essentially didn't exist.

The owners and management drummed up anti-union sentiment with a paternalistic approach, working the term 'NFL family' to death. 'No Freedom, No Football' became the striking players' battle cry. The strike lasted forty-four days. Things came to a head on 27 July, when players picketed the Hall of Fame Game in Canton. By 10 August, the owners still had not agreed to a single demand. Finally, in frustration, the players called off the strike. They took the battle to the courts in a standoff that lasted more than three seasons. But each time the NFLPA was victorious in court, the owners seemed to find a loophole. Real free agency wouldn't arrive until 1993.

8

One player became synonymous with the term 'free agent' in the 1990s: Deion Sanders. He was an all-round athlete in the Jim Thorpe mold, lettering in baseball, football, and basketball at his high-school in Fort Myers, Florida. As a senior, Sanders was drafted by the Kansas City Royals, but he turned down professional baseball to play college football – alongside baseball and track – at Florida State University (FSU). The Seminoles, Bobby Bowden's team, were emerging as one of the top teams in the country. Sanders had played quarterback and safety in high school, but FSU recruited him as a cornerback – a thankless position, designated to shut down wide receivers. But Sanders wasn't about to be relegated, no matter what position he played. He showed out before long. As a true freshman, Sanders returned a punt and an interception for touchdowns. His sophomore year he upped that to four interceptions in eleven games played. He did the same his junior year. His senior year he had five interceptions, with one returned for a touchdown. He developed into a skilled route-jumper and shutdown corner. He could play man-to-man coverage against any team's number-one receiver and give as good as he got. He was one of the most exciting kick returners ever to play the game. To see him run with the ball, it made you wonder why they didn't just give him the ball every play. He was so fast – who could catch him?

Deion was never not about getting paid, and he knew where being humble got you. He had been overlooked before. FSU hadn't wanted him at quarterback. They'd wanted him to play corner. They weren't thinking about what he could earn in the NFL as a quarterback compared to as a corner. Cornerback was among the least financially lucrative positions in football. Sanders had seen the data and knew that it'd be a problem for him when (not if) the NFL drafted him. So he came up with a solution to that problem, and that solution was a persona: Prime Time.

Prime Time – just Prime, to his friends – wasn't exactly Deion Sanders. Unlike Deion Sanders, Prime was ostentatious. Prime was loud. Prime was flashy. Prime wore expensive clothes, expensive sunglasses, gold chains, Jheri curl. Prime said things like: 'Water covers two-thirds of the Earth. I cover the rest.' When it was pointed out that he neglected to do warm-up exercises, he came back with: 'When have you seen a cheetah stretch before you go get the antelope?' The point was to present success to attract success.

The idea was a winner. In the 1989 NFL draft, Sanders went number five overall to the Atlanta Falcons. But he wanted more money than they offered, more than twice as much as the cornerback picked fifth the year before. The difference between that cornerback and Sanders was that Sanders had a second pro sport he could fall back on. He'd been drafted by the New York Yankees in 1988 (how he'd got his gold-chain budget). The Yankees had taken an interest in Sanders's speed, as they were looking for a leadoff hitter to take the place of Rickey Henderson, who'd stolen a hundred bases a year for them before they traded him to the Oakland Athletics. When the Falcons didn't want to pay Prime what Prime thought Prime was worth, Prime could afford to sit out a year; Prime could do a lot worse than play outfield for the New York Yankees.

So Sanders held out. The Yankees had called him up from the minors in the summer of 1989. They saw an opportunity to give Deion a sample of what it was like playing in 'the show'. They thought they might tempt him away from the NFL. Deion dutifully let the Falcons know about it. He held out until 7 September, when the Falcons agreed to terms. The way it played out, the Falcons didn't look like idiots for paying Sanders more than twice what the fifth pick got paid the year before.

In Sanders's first regular season game in the NFL, he returned a punt sixty-eight yards for a touchdown. Earlier that week he hit a home run in a game for the Yankees. Not even Jim Thorpe had ever hit an MLB home run and scored an NFL touchdown in the same week. Prime Time's stock was going up.

Having secured his $4.4 million from the Falcons, he was less accommodating to the Yankees. He began negotiations for more money. He wanted $1 million a year, but the Yankees weren't having that. Sanders was still growing as a hitter. Owner George Steinbrenner didn't want to pay a major contract to a developing player. The Yankee front office worried that giving Sanders a high-dollar contract would sow division in the locker room. It's likely that Sanders didn't want to play for the Yankees anymore and was looking for an exit. He had probably known it wasn't going to work out when he looked to see where he might land in the NFL draft, and saw the New York teams, the Jets and the Giants, were sitting on picks fourteen and eighteen respectively, neither pick anywhere near high enough to draft him. Like he told the Giants, he'd be gone by then.

9

The story went: Sanders had begged the Falcons organization to draft him. Which was odd, since the Falcons were in the conversation for the worst franchise in the NFL. They had one playoff win in their entire history, in the wild-card round. But the only teams with top-ten picks that shared a city with a Major League Baseball team were Detroit, Kansas City, Atlanta, and Pittsburgh – the number three, four, five, and seven picks, respectively. The Lions were going to pick Barry Sanders, a future Hall of Fame running back out of Oklahoma State. Kansas City was a non-starter because the Royals had drafted Sanders out of high school and he had blown them off to play football – not to mention Kansas City might be a little crowded for Sanders, what with another famous two-sport athlete there, Royals slugger and LA Raiders running back Bo Jackson.

Pittsburgh would've been the best NFL franchise Sanders could have landed with, at least in terms of a winning tradition. The Steelers had won more NFL championships than any other team in the Super Bowl era; but the problem with Prime Time going to Pittsburgh was the Pittsburgh Pirates weren't in the market for an outfielder, as at the time they had as good an outfield as any ever: Barry Bonds, Bobby Bonilla, Moisés Alou. Atlanta was the only viable option Sanders had if he wanted to play football and baseball in the same city. Beyond that, the city of Atlanta had certain advantages. Atlanta's baseball team, the Braves, were owned by Ted Turner, a billionaire back when that sort of thing was rare. Turner owned the Cable News Network, Turner Network Television, and Turner Broadcasting System – three national cable channels, one of which, TBS, televised every single Atlanta Braves regular season game coast to coast. The New York Yankees couldn't even offer that. For a young Prime Time on the grind, trying to build his brand in professional sports, that kind of promotion was a gold mine.

10

Despite the individual success Sanders had on the field in 1989, the Falcons overall didn't fare well, ending the year 3–13. Yet there were reasons to be optimistic. The team had a promising young quarterback, Chris Miller, and had traded a first-round pick in that year's NFL draft to the Indianapolis Colts to get Miller some more help at the wide receiver position in the form of Andre Rison. He would complement wide receiver Michael Haynes. It was hard to imagine a defense being able to shut down both. The team had a new head coach, too: Jerry Glanville, who was hired by Atlanta a week after he was fired by Houston, where he'd had a controversial tenure as head coach of the Oilers.

Glanville was a man accustomed to getting death threats. On occasion, he would wear a bulletproof vest on the sidelines. They said if you saw him with his high-plains-drifter jacket on it meant he had the vest strapped on him underneath. All that was well and fine, but where things had really gone wrong in Houston was his lack of concern about the extenuating consequences of his feuding. Houston's franchise quarterback Warren Moon took issue with Glanville putting a target on his players. Glanville talked tough but he didn't have to walk the walk on the field, was the jist of Moon's complaint. Humbled and perhaps more self-aware, Glanville came to Atlanta. He asked the team's ownership to change the players' uniforms. Like Prime Time, Jerry Glanville had his own persona – 'the man in black' – and he wanted his team's uniforms to fit the persona. He had tried to get the Oilers to change their uniforms to all black, but the ownership had rejected the idea. He had better luck in Atlanta. Regardless of his poor playoff record, he had won twice as many playoff games as the team had in its entire history. So they humored him.

Glanville and Sanders seemed an ideal match. Sanders was never a cheap-shot artist or a dirty player, but both men were believers in the power of aura. With longtime head coach Marion Campbell gone, there was a chance for Sanders to assert his own aura in the locker room. Glanville, a fan of hype, was a fan of Deion and recognized the value he brought to the team, not just as a player but as a leader. After a lackluster first year, the Falcons began to find a winning formula.

These were Sanders's halcyon days. He loved Atlanta, and the feeling was mostly mutual. He signed with the Atlanta Braves and, that summer, helped them to go from worst to first in the National League, when he filled in for Braves center fielder Otis Nixon, during Nixon's suspension for drug use. And in 1991, the Falcons began at last to put it together. They were 'the rudest team in the NFL'. Glanville always wanted to be seen as running with the bad boys, and now he was.

Sanders developed a close relationship with recording artist MC Hammer, who was at the peak of his popularity. In September

1991, Hammer released a new single '2 Legit 2 Quit' – a song he recorded in honor of Prime Time and the Atlanta Falcons. The single sold five million copies and became the Falcons' team anthem that year. Hammer was Sanders's guest on the sidelines at every game, an unofficial member of the team. Glanville and Sanders, whether they admitted to one another or not, subscribed to very similar philosophies: hype was a tool you could use. Sanders famously distilled his motto in the lines: 'If you look good you play good. If you play good you get paid good.'

When Sanders became Prime Time, he was taking a great risk. If he hadn't delivered on the field, he would've looked ridiculous. To talk noise like Prime talked noise and then fail to show up for the game – death might be preferable to such humiliation. When you said so loudly that you were the best, that you were worth the top dollar, then not just every game but every play became important, because you could never slip, you always had to back it up. Every game was a championship game when you were telling everybody you were the champ. When you do that, though, there is always a chance you'll fall flat. You'll burn out. This was the fate of the Atlanta Falcons of the early 1990s. And it was almost the fate of Deion Sanders.

11

The high-water mark came in the wild-card round of the 1991 playoffs, when the Falcons went to the Superdome in New Orleans and disrespected their rival, the Saints, beating them 27–20. The Falcons were riding high. They were the hottest team in the league, having won five of their last six games (they'd won four of their last five in the regular season to finish at a worthy 10–6). VIPs milled around their sidelines: Hammer, Evander Holyfield, Travis Tritt (the country-music star was Glanville's buddy), even James Brown. The only problem was the team as a whole wasn't that solid. They had good players: Sanders, Miller, Rison, Jessie Tuggle, to name a few. But they hadn't had time to build depth around their core, not enough to compete with the top teams in the NFL. There wasn't a lot of playoff experience in the locker room. Too much of the focus had been on what was going right, on Sanders and Rison, former college rivals, now best friends – Prime Time and Showtime.

But the Falcons couldn't stop the run. And then Glanville benched the team's leading rusher, running back Mike Rozier, for the divisional round of the playoffs. Rozier had missed the flight to Washington, and then missed the 10 p.m. bed check at the team's hotel the night before the game. Rozier had followed Glanville from Houston to Atlanta, and Glanville repaid his loyalty by taking him out of the game, even though he was the most productive running back that Glanville had and the conditions (monsoon) were not favorable to the passing game. The Falcons were unable to run the ball, allowing the ten-point favorites of Washington to sit back and watch the Falcons' wideouts struggle for purchase in the deluge pouring into RFK stadium.

A divisional playoff loss on the road in Washington to the team that ended up winning the Super Bowl – this wasn't the end of the world. But things began to fall apart, both for the team and for Deion. There were players who blamed Glanville for their humiliation. They thought Glanville should've been a grown-up about it and played Rozier. Rozier may have fucked up, but the playoffs were the playoffs. Glanville could've suspended him later. He picked a bad time to start looking down on bad-boy behavior. Wasn't he supposed to be a party guy?

Deion went about his business. The dream would last a bit longer, but the events that would bring it to an end were already in motion. Tensions were growing between the Falcons and the Braves over who had Sanders's ultimate loyalty. Football was Sanders's wife; baseball, his girlfriend. But the Braves had made it to the World Series, whereas the Falcons was a team that had been beat down in the mud in front of their celebrity entourage.

It was one of the most brutal eras of NFL football. Teams were playing on Astroturf, which was the same as playing on concrete, only with concrete the abrasions one got wouldn't be as bad. Players were getting carted off every weekend, never to return to the field. Helmet-to-helmet hits were SOP. Guys were still looking to knock people out. The Atlanta Braves were wary of investing too heavily in a player who might be incapacitated in the off-season. But when they looked at Sanders they saw Rickey Henderson with better power, not to mention that Sanders was good for the bottom line. He was a publicity factory. People would come just to see him play. Meanwhile, the lines began to blur for Sanders. He had been around long enough not to be overawed or deferential. He had been careful in the beginning, code-switching between the baseball world and the football world. Prime didn't play baseball. Deion Sanders played baseball. But the more his celebrity grew, the harder it was to separate Prime from the baseball diamond.

Some of it was miscommunication, willful or otherwise. Sanders was getting playing time with the Braves, and he was performing well. He was showing signs of coming into his own as a hitter. Defensively, he was a solid outfielder. What he lacked in experience (like, say, how well he could read the ball coming off of the bat), he made up for in natural ability, and he could steal bases. If he got on base at all it was like hitting a double. Even if he didn't steal bases, just his presence on first base could throw a pitcher off.

Things began to come to a head in the summer of 1992, when the Falcons offered Deion an extra million dollars if he ditched the Braves early so he could be with the team at training camp. The offer made headlines, Deion turned it down, and the only thing that came of it was an increase in frustration for all parties involved. In baseball, bringing attention to success wasn't always a good thing. To illustrate: while in football it was acceptable to celebrate a play – be it a touchdown, a quarterback sack, an interception – you wouldn't get away with it in baseball. Say you hit a home run in a game, if the other team thought you'd stayed and watched the ball too long when it came off the bat, your next time at the plate the pitcher was going to throw the ball at you, hard, and maybe at your head. Baseball was a game of subtlety.

It hit the fan in October. Deion had agreed to terms with the Braves under which he would be available to play for them in the postseason, should they make it to the postseason, which they did. They ended up playing the Pirates, in Pittsburgh, for the National League pennant, the same weekend the Falcons were scheduled to play the Miami Dolphins in Miami. The Braves told him they expected him to stay with the team the whole time. Deion indicated he was going to play for both teams that weekend. The Braves disagreed with his interpretation of their agreement, namely his interpretation of the meaning of 'full time' – Prime Time took it to mean that it was like the meaning of full-time as in a full-time job, whereby you have to work when you're scheduled to work, but that you're not beholden to be any specific place when you aren't working. By Sanders's interpretation, it stood to reason that he could play for the Braves in Pittsburgh on Saturday night, catch a plane to Miami that night, play in the Falcons' game that Sunday, then go straight to the airport and fly back to Pittsburgh for the Braves' game that night. He could charter a jet. Nike would help him put it together. CBS was interested in tagging along for the ride. Deion thought he was doing good, like he was coming to somebody's rescue. It all seemed entirely reasonable to him. When Sanders got back to Pittsburgh, he rolled in around game time. He suited up but he didn't play. The Braves let him sit on the bench.

The Braves lost that night. But they won the series in seven games, and they advanced to their second World Series in two years. They couldn't keep Deion out of the starting lineup. He led the team with eight hits. Most of the rest of the Braves didn't show up. Which was ironic. They were there, but they weren't *there*. Deion, on the other hand, was there, and even missed a Falcons game to be there. But it didn't matter. The well was poisoned. The Braves' owner John Schuerholz was a highly competent general manager, but also kind of a prick. How much of a prick? Schuerholz traded Sanders in about the coldest way possible – to the Cincinnati Reds. Which, if you knew anything about Major League Baseball, meant you were getting owned. The thing they said about the Reds' owner Marge Schott was that she was a fan of Hitler, wore Nazi armbands when at home, and when at work, was said to drop the hard-r casually. And it got cold in Cincinnati. Not Cleveland cold, not Green Bay cold. But colder than Sanders would've liked. Deion was from Florida. And they already had a Sanders on the Reds. Reggie Sanders. Who was a great player. And probably he and Deion were friends. At least I always assumed they were. But damn.

Atlanta was Deion's city. It was like if the Bulls traded Michael Jordan or the Lakers traded Magic Johnson or the Celtics traded Larry Bird. It was like if the Bears traded Walter Payton. Granted, Deion wasn't as vital to the Braves as any of those were to the above. But to the city, a city that had national aspirations, as in being a city that somebody not from there might give a fuck about, Deion Sanders was vital.

The Falcons flaked on him, too. They'd been winning in 1991. In 1992 they weren't winning anymore. Chris Miller went down with a season-ending injury and needed knee surgery. Deion missed games. The offense struggled. The defense couldn't stop the run. Glanville was looking bad, and like anybody else would, Jerry Glanville blamed people around him for fucking up his shit. Deion was not immune. He was no longer the heart and soul of the Atlanta roster. He was labeled a distraction, more trouble than he was worth. He wasn't offered a new contract.

12

The dissolution of the Prime Time Falcons set Atlanta back years. Deion left for the San Francisco 49ers and you saw him trade blows with Andre Rison in the Georgia Dome in 1994, on TV. They both got fined $7,500. Deion and the Niners won the Super Bowl that year. Then Deion left for Dallas and won a Super Bowl for the Cowboys the season after that. He never played for Atlanta again. Atlanta still hasn't won a Super Bowl. Deion retired in 2006.

In 2020 Deion Sanders made his foray into coaching college ball. It began at Jackson State University (JSU) after a 'strategic call from God'. Clearly he wasn't motivated by money. Sanders's salary at JSU was $300,000 a year, a fraction of what he could've made as a TV analyst, and half of that salary he donated back to the school to put toward the renovation of its football stadium. Sanders coached three seasons at JSU. The first year the team went 4–3, in a season shortened by the 2020 pandemic. Sanders's second year at JSU was a turn-around year for the program, with the JSU Tigers going 11–2 in 2021 and then 12–1 in 2022.

Two years ago, after another call from the Almighty, Sanders became head coach of one of the worst teams in one of the whitest college towns in America: the Buffaloes of Boulder, Colorado. CU Boulder was a football backwater when Coach Prime arrived. The last time the school won a national title was 1990. In 2022, Colorado won one game, losing eight and finishing dead last in their conference. The athletic director of the school, Rick George, couldn't see a downside in taking a chance on Coach Prime.

It wasn't much of a gamble. Sanders brought with him two of the best players in college football: his son, quarterback Shedeur Sanders, and wide receiver/defensive back Travis Hunter. They came to Colorado via the transfer from JSU. Despite winning four times as many games as the team did the year before, Sanders was, not surprisingly, criticized. It was said he wasn't 'really a head coach', but more like a 'producer', someone who made things look good, but who wasn't serious about winning. This only raised the question: what is the college coach's priority: to win a championship or to try to get as many players as possible into the pros? You can't eat a national championship trophy. When Travis Hunter was left off the list of candidates for the Jim Thorpe trophy, Deion promised to give him his own.

13

A football man is in the White House again. In 1984, Donald J. Trump became owner of the New Jersey Generals, a professional team in a then-newly-founded USFL, the United States Football League. By then, the New York property mogul and future POTUS had twice tried and failed to acquire an NFL team, the Baltimore Colts, in 1981 and 1983. He offered Colts owner Robert Irsay $50 million twice, and twice Irsay had turned him down. When he bought the New Jersey Generals, he inherited Herschel Walker, a Heisman Trophy-winning running back and second-year pro. He also inherited a team that played its games in the spring. Which Trump, as a sports fan, found sacrilegious. In his second year as owner he led a revolt of the USFL ownership, whom he convinced to go against the NFL head-on, to schedule their football games to be played in the fall like everybody else.

Of the league's owners, Trump was the most active in the media, making his importance as an owner outsized. The other owners, in turn, followed him to the league's destruction, all in what was no more than a ploy by Trump to coerce the NFL into a merger. Trump's motive was not long in being laid bare. Trump enlisted attorney Roy Cohn to help bring a suit against the NFL, in the hopes that, on grounds the NFL had illegally colluded with the three major US TV networks (ABC, CBS, and NBC) to freeze the USFL out of the national market, the US government would compel the NFL to merge with Trump's USFL. Trump's game was transparent, his tact so lacking that NFL Commissioner Pete Rozelle vowed that as long as he lived Donald Trump would not own an NFL franchise, a vow that held good when Trump failed to acquire the Dallas Cowboys in 1988.

Pete Rozelle died in 1996. Trump made a bid in 2014 to buy the Buffalo Bills. It was a deal Trump couldn't close. It's been said he couldn't come up with a sufficient line of credit. He was reported to have offered a billion. The team sold for $1.4 billion. Shut out again,

Trump would have to settle for running for the highest office in the land, winning, against all odds, the 2016 US presidential election. The rest is well known.

Trump wasn't done with football, though. He still likes to attend Southeastern Conference games. The crowds are well-disposed to him. And football remains the lifeblood of the Republican Party. From 2016 Republicans began to take issue with the fact that the NFL charged the military for ads. They don't anymore. Flags. Blitz. CTE. Lockheed Martin. One and the same. Lights, camera, action.

It's said the game's not as violent as it used to be. If that's true, it is for the best. The game is still violent enough. It's violent enough and yet the rules let the quarterback live a little while longer, when the position used to be like a spot on death row. In other respects, things stayed the same. We still render to the dollar. Once more the season is over. It doesn't matter who won the trophy or who the president is, the massacres will continue. We have lost count of how many we've committed since 9/11. If there's a God in heaven, America will burn to the ground one day. Until then, there is football. ∎

Edited by James L W West III with
an introduction by Sarah Churchwell

THE CAMBRIDGE CENTENNIAL EDITION OF

The GREAT
GATSBY

F. SCOTT
FITZGERALD

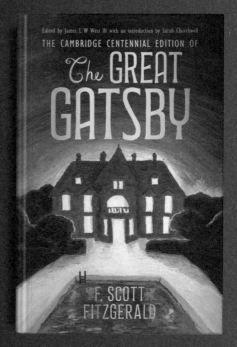

9781009414593 | Hardback | January 2025 | £20

cambridge.org/GreatGatsby100

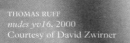

ROUND ONE

Benjamin Nugent

Luke was forty-five years old, and in all his life he'd almost never viewed pornography in any form. There had been a year in his late twenties, a time of professional failure, in which he'd developed a fondness for a photo on *Playboy*'s landing page: a woman in the shower, adorned with suds wrung from her loofah. But that was it. He was never tempted to give it another try. He never asked his wife, Rita, to describe the videos she watched in her study with the door closed and her earbuds in. He rarely spoke of his abjuration because he didn't want to lord it over anyone, and because he doubted any of his friends would believe him.

Once, he mentioned it to his best friend Elijah, while they were cooking dinner in an Airbnb in the Catskills. Their wives had taken the car to a meditation class at a hillside ashram. He half expected Elijah to say something like, *I never look at it either, this whole myth about male porn consumption is bullshit.* But Elijah's face darkened. He scraped the seeds from a bell pepper and refused to meet Luke's eyes. To show Elijah he wasn't bragging, Luke said, 'I'm five years older than you, and my parents are hippies, so I didn't have internet when I was in high school. I'm not saying I have superior willpower. I'm just lucky I didn't get hooked when I was a kid.' Elijah did not dignify this remark with a response.

Maybe Luke was bragging. Sometimes, running in the park, he wondered if he was the last of a dying breed. Over the years, a few different women he'd dated had told him his disinterest in porn was unusual and endearing. Those compliments had confirmed that his rejection of porn was more than a personal choice, something more like a talent, an asset. Then, early in his courtship with Rita, she said, 'I feel like your not watching porn is why you like my body so much and why you have sex slightly differently from other guys.' He wished it were feasible to tattoo that statement on his neck. In moments of distress – when he missed a fundraising goal at work or glanced at a bank statement – he whispered it to himself, like a prayer. Looking at porn became as unimaginable as shoplifting, or going to business school, an act that would undermine his sense of self.

One morning, when Rita was nearing the end of her first round of IVF, she reminded him, over breakfast, that on the day the doctors extracted the eggs from her ovaries, he would have to go into a room in the hospital and produce. Last month he'd produced the sample for his semen analysis at home, put the sterile cup in a tote bag, and delivered it to the clinic. But this time was going to be different. Weill Cornell rules dictated that all production for purposes of fertilization, as opposed to testing, take place on site, right before the woman went under twilight anesthesia.

Luke drank down his orange juice. 'It's weird they don't send couples into the room together, given what they need the guy to do.'

'I never thought about that,' said Rita. 'That is weird.' Suddenly, she looked concerned. 'You realize,' she said, 'there's going to be porn in the room.'

'Of course. Who cares?' The truth was, he hadn't thought about it. But he wasn't worried. It wasn't as if he never masturbated. He just thought about Rita and his ex-girlfriends when he did it, and he could do that in the presence of a blank computer screen. Compared to what Rita was going through, his job was so easy it wasn't a job. She had to: inject herself every evening with multiple medications, including Menopur, an ovary stimulant whose active ingredient was distilled from the urine of post-menopausal women; refrain from exercise; and walk around all day with ovaries so swollen she could feel them jounce. And that was to say nothing of her psychological burden. Their insurance didn't cover IVF; Rita was a therapist in private practice and Luke worked for an ocean-conservation nonprofit whose employee association had given up fertility assistance, among other benefits, in exchange for flexible hours and a permissive work-from-home policy. To pay for round one, he'd raided his 403(b), Rita her 401(k). A round two would mean either the hunnish sacking of those accounts or the assumption of debt and the death of the dream of home ownership. A round three was out of the question. The prospect of a childless life did not appall Luke. It sounded empty and free. But for Rita, it was the stuff of nightmares. One early morning last month she'd gasped and bolted upright in bed. He'd asked her what she'd been dreaming about.

'Not being able to have a baby.'

The next day, a sonogram revealed that the follicles housing Rita's oocytes had grown to auspicious size. It was time to trigger ovulation. That night, she drew a circle in black marker high on her left buttock and Luke knelt behind her, jabbed her with a long-needled syringe, holding it like a pencil, and drove home the plunger with his thumb, pushing the chemicals through the barrel into her muscle.

Thirty-five hours later, they were in the waiting room. Rita wore a pre-op robe, non-slip socks, a surgical cap, and hospital pajamas two sizes too large for her. A nurse escorted a man Luke's age down the hall to The Room, and the man returned ten minutes later. The nurse escorted another man Luke's age down the hall, and this man took longer to produce, about fifteen minutes. Finally, she called Luke's name. He squeezed Rita's hand and followed the nurse down the corridor.

The nurse was stone-faced and silent as she swiped a card against a reader on the wall. The doors at the end of the corridor swung open to welcome them into a secure inner sanctum of the fertility wing. She turned left, opened another door with a key, stepped into a dim chamber, and beckoned.

The room was the size of a cubicle. A urinal was bolted to one of the yellow cinderblock walls. To the right of the urinal there was a paper-towel dispenser, to the left a sink and a mirror. On a fake marble countertop, left of the sink, stood a monitor that displayed a menu of six videos, represented by six still frames of men and women captured in the midst of sexual acts, each option with a title: *COMBAT ZONE*; *MOTHERLOAD FACIALS*; *DOUBLE-PENETRATION BLONDES*; *BLONDE AMBITION*; *19-YO CUM-LICKERS*; *BLONDE ASS-BANG*. 'Videos,' said his Virgil, gesturing with her gloved hand, touching nothing. She indicated a rack of capped vials. 'Lube.' She pointed to a blue leatherette recliner facing the monitor. 'The chair.' The recliner's seat was covered with a large rectangular pad, made of disposable, absorbent, synthetic cloth. 'Magazines,' she said, pointing to a low, black, filing cabinet. 'When you're done, look at the time.' On the digital wall clock, hours and minutes were eight inches high. Seconds flashed away in miniature. 'Record the time of production on the label of the cup.' She placed the sample cup beside a jar of pens. 'Once you've recorded the production time, put the cup in here.' She showed him a safe embedded in the wall, and a red button to push when he was ready to return to the waiting room. He thanked her. She left and shut the door, leaving him alone with the computer.

Dazed by the violence of the still images drawn from the videos, he treated the monitor like a touch screen, pressing on the menu icon with his index finger to try to make the pictures disappear. In a way, they belonged here, in this house of appendectomies, biopsies, shunts, and debridement. Every vulva was shaved bare. The two anuses were wide open, one filled with a cock, the other empty, a black hole. The women's mouths, too, were agape, as if for intubation. The faces of the men were the faces of surgeons at their work, detached and focused, and the light was the light of an operating room, every fold and vein illuminated. Finally, he found a remote on the counter. He hit what looked like a power button several times and soon the pictures were gone, replaced by a night shot of the Manhattan skyline.

He turned on the cold water, washed his face, pissed in the urinal, and washed his hands. He washed his face again and ran the cold water through his hair. It was possible that the man who'd used this facility before him, the fifteen-minute guy, was a perv. Maybe the images on the screen reflected his personal search history and idiosyncratic taste, rather than the default choices to which the menu reverted. There was no reason to despair of the human race. There were all kinds of people out there. Everyone knew that porn, these days, fed every conceivable appetite. And of course he'd known that a lot of porn was brutal and degrading. But there was a difference between knowing this to be true and seeing it. The shock would not have been a big deal, really, but for the time-sensitive nature of the task before him. There were seven or eight other couples in the waiting room, each with their own slot on the schedule. Every woman needed to go into surgery thirty-six hours after her ovulation trigger and required the semen of her male collaborator. He could not hold up the works. He would overcome this ridiculous blow to his faith in the goodness of others, and provide.

He stripped, sat on the absorbent pad, and closed his eyes. He put his hands between his legs. It felt like rubbing his ear. He tried to remember the loud, low sound one of his ex-girlfriends made when she came. Okay: this was the beginning of arousal, modest progress. But his memory of the stills from the videos was a floodlight that blotted out the stars. His little erection seemed almost to recoil as it contracted and fell. He could hear the traffic of nurses in the corridor. He looked at the big digital numbers. Five minutes had passed.

Why was it that he couldn't forget his glimpse of *COMBAT ZONE, MOTHERLOAD FACIALS*, and the rest of the collection? Maybe this was how people got addicted to porn in the first place; its violence, its car-crash quality, was there to make it indelible. If the stills had been tableaux of lovers engaged in humane, mutual gratification, they would have been easier to banish from the mind.

Seven minutes had passed. He thought of the cash they'd dropped on this round, thirty-one thousand dollars on the line. Maybe he was thrown by the images from the porn because they played on his most shameful fantasies. *This thing of darkness I acknowledge mine*, he thought, striving to unleash and nurture some heretofore chastised inner frat bro. Still, no stirring in the loins. Thirty-one thousand dollars was a vast understatement if you considered how the money would have multiplied over decades, had it remained in mutual funds, where it belonged. Ten minutes had passed. The foot traffic outside sounded closer to the door than ever, and he wondered if the nurses were circling, ready to give him a five-minute warning. Nobody knocked. But he knew the nurses and the other men were out there. They were depending on him to get it done and leave.

He stood and looked at his naked body in the mirror. He concocted elaborate fantasies, of sacramental sex, ceremonies in tents. In a few minutes, he was hard. But the expression that came over his face when he imagined himself partaking in an ancient ritual reminded him of the scowl of the ogre in *BLONDE AMBITION*. Once more, he watched a fledgling erection flag in his hand. He lowered himself back onto the pad. Fifteen minutes had passed, and then twenty.

He was stalling the rotation of men through the room to such a degree that he was almost certainly reducing other couples' chances of conception. His penis was raw and cowering, his progress negative. He varied his movements and tried to empty his mind. Now thirty minutes had passed. Why was he so unmanned by his glimpse of what other men liked? Perhaps if he could understand the reason the still frames had robbed him of his potency, he could wrest his potency back. The problem, he speculated, was that he liked to feel superior to other men. That was why his dick would not stoop so low as to respond positively to porn, as an average dick would. Turning up its nose at coarse, misogynistic imagery, that is, at the peasant fare upon which average dicks feasted, was an assertion of its refined, aristocratic nature. Now that he had figured out what was going on, maybe he could be a dick-whisperer. He literally whispered, to his dick and to himself, 'There's nothing wrong with being like everybody else. There's nothing wrong with being like everybody else.' But the fact was, he did think there was something wrong with it. He couldn't get turned on by the still frames because, deep down, he didn't want to be turned on by them. And yet he could not push them out of his head. Forty minutes.

The time had come to face facts. It was a terrible thing. But it would do no good to pretend the situation was otherwise. His hands trembled as he picked up his belt, with its once-fashionable rodeo buckle, and laced his boots.

When he pushed open the door of the waiting room, Rita waved, and held out an arm to welcome him. He sat beside her on one of the plastic chairs and took her hand.

'I'm sorry,' he said. 'I couldn't do it.'

She wore an N-95 because she was worried that if she caught Covid, or the flu, or a cold, it would compromise her fertility. The only exposed part of her face was her eyes. She blinked, twice.

'Sweetie,' she said. 'You haven't done it yet. But you're going to do it now.'

He released her hand, stared at the floor, and scratched the back of his neck.

'I believe in you,' she said, sounding desolate and frightened. 'You're going to get back in there, and you're not going to come back out until you're finished.'

'All of these people,' he said, 'are waiting to go. They need the room, too.'

'Which is why you need to go back right now, before the nurses think you're done and send in somebody else.'

'But I've taken too much time already. I can't do anything at all.'

'Is it the porn?' she asked.

He nodded. 'They left it on the screen.'

'Okay,' she said. 'I can see how that would be weird for you. I know that you're pure in certain ways. It's one of the reasons I love you. But you need to get turned on, any way you can. Have you tried using the porn?'

He shook his head.

'I think you should try it. You need to find a way to have fun in there.' She stroked his hair. 'I know that it's a new thing for you. But I think that if you keep an open mind, you're going to have fun.'

He took a deep breath. He focused on the soothing touch of her hand. 'Fun.'

'That's right,' she said. 'Can you try to have fun? Will you do that for me?'

'I'm going to do it,' he said. 'I'm going to have a good time.'

She seized the arm of a passing nurse. 'He needs to try again,' she said.

B ack in the room, he took off his clothes and resettled himself on the crinkling pad. It was a matter of turning into a different person for a few minutes. He pulled open the drawer of the cabinet full of magazines. On the top of the pile lay *Just Barely 18*. The cover girl, who wore a thong, braced herself against a gymnasium wall, turning to regard the viewer with a guileless expression that emphasized her status as a child. He threw it on the floor and looked at the next one, *Barely Legal*. He wondered if *Barely Legal* had ever brought an intellectual property case against *Just Barely 18*. He threw it on the floor. Next was *Hustler*, which was like the video stills, in print form. He threw it on the floor, and it skidded over the others. Beneath *Hustler*, at the bottom of the pile, lay a hard-used *Playboy*, its cover torn off.

The Girl of the Big Ten, a brunette, hailed from Wisconsin. She was corn-fed, wholesome. Naked on her stomach, casual, on a nondescript bed, she was propped up on her elbows in the fashion of a person reading a book or scrolling on a phone. She regarded the camera with an indulgent, irritable smile. All the other women in the magazine were odalisques, but this one attended an excellent land-grant university, and her attitude was one of thinly veiled disdain.

Her posture and face reminded him of Rita's disposition after an argument. And so in his imaginary coupling with the Girl, they had recently argued, and sex was their way of beating swords into plowshares.

'It's okay,' she said, with her wry mouth, her arched eyebrows. 'I know you get stressed about work sometimes. And then you get dark. But I don't care. It's because you work so hard. There are so few people at the good NGOs who are so fucking good at operations and strategy. When I really think about it, I don't think there's anyone who's as good at them as you are. It's true you fucked up, a little, in this room, today. But I fuck up sometimes, too. I'll admit that. I'm driven to be so good. Sometimes I get so dark, just like you.' And she assured him, over and over, for five minutes, that it felt good to fuck, because he was so good, the best in the world, at everything she cared about, and because he made her life better with his competence.

The climax was so feeble it barely took place, but it sent him into ecstasies of relief. He and Rita were going to have a baby. It might have her red hair, her wide nose, her narrow eyes. Or, if they didn't have a baby, it would not be his fault. He screwed the lid onto the cup and committed the hour and minute to the label in a faint, trembling hand. The numbers looked as if they'd been written by a stranger.

Two hours later Rita was released from the hospital. They walked to the subway with her hand on his arm, slow, almost shuffling. Her ovaries hurt, and her cramps were getting worse as the fentanyl wore off, but she was elated. The doctor had harvested ten eggs, a good haul, considering Rita's age. It was likely that half would fertilize, and half of those would grow to blastocysts. Of the two or three likely blastocysts, it was probable that one would test genetically normal, and thus qualify for transfer to her uterus. Once implanted there, it would have a 65 percent chance of resulting in pregnancy. She rattled off these odds, already a specialist in the field.

She spoke of the future. In two weeks, she'd be allowed to exercise and have sex again. But not for long. If they were lucky, the transfer would take place in a little more than a month, and then she'd have to be careful, in deference to her age and the delicacy of the first trimester.

'I knew porn was pretty fucked up, but I didn't realize how fucked up,' he said.

'Yeah,' she said. 'To find attractive people, I usually have to look at terrible shit. Did you know that the women sometimes surgically remove part of their labia?'

'The genitals didn't look like real genitals.'

'What did you watch to get off? You don't have to tell me if you don't want to.'

He told her.

'That's not even porn.'

'What's *Playboy* if not porn?'

'What people mean by porn these days is different from that. With a video, it can surprise you. Last week I was watching what seemed like shitty, heterosexual, anal-sex porn, and I assumed the woman was faking it, and then she started touching herself and shaking, and it was like, *Holy shit, I think she's really having an orgasm.* Other times, I've been having a decent experience, and suddenly I've looked at the woman more closely, and been like, *Oh my God, am I watching a person getting raped?*'

'When we have sex, and you tell me your fantasies, are they from porn?' he asked.

'Sometimes.' She studied his face, amused. 'You're getting an education. You look a little traumatized.' They rode an escalator down a long way underground, and then another one even deeper. On the train, a woman walked from car to car selling candy from a cardboard box, saying 'chicle, chocolate' over and over in a quiet voice. She had a boy in tow, four or five years old. Twice, he knelt on the seats and tugged at a strap of her backpack, calling to her in vain.

The next day was bright and very cold. The tiny mounds of snow on the sidewalk were hard and glimmering. Luke stepped over patches of ice on his way to the bakery. At eleven o'clock that morning, Rita looked at a number on her phone and picked up. She paced and covered her free ear. The only sound she made was an occasional 'okay'. She said thank you, hung up, and stared at the wall.

'Who was that?'

She looked at him for a moment before she spoke. 'Only two of them fertilized.'

They sat at the dining-room table. She was hunched as if ill.

'What's going to happen?' he asked.

'Maybe we'll get one blastocyst. But, if we do, it probably won't be genetically normal, because most of them aren't, when you're my age. So, nothing.' She went into the bedroom, kicked off her shoes, and lay on her back with her hands over her eyes.

He followed her in, and held the balls of her feet, in their threadbare socks. She spoke of the grief she felt for the baby girl she'd imagined, and tried to visualize her fading and disappearing, like a ghost, so she wouldn't think about her anymore.

'We did everything we could have done,' he said.

'Did we? I'm not sure that's true. If you'd been able to jerk off without panicking, things might have been different. Stress affects sperm quality. I googled it, but I didn't tell you, because I didn't want to stress you out about getting stressed.'

'Obviously,' he said, 'they mean stress over days, and weeks, and months. But, I mean, yeah, the orgasm was really bad. The cup looked like a gnome had jizzed in it.'

'You know what? I don't find that funny right now. I find that upsetting. There was a study where men who took longer than twenty minutes to produce made fewer viable sperm than other men. So I'm not sure what to say to you.'

'You're making me feel like shit,' he said. 'You're forty-one. That's the problem.'

She lifted her hands and sat up. 'I made ten eggs.'

'Wow. Ten fucked-up, middle-aged ovary eggs that have little to no hope of ever becoming a human being. You must be really proud of yourself.'

'I'm glad we're doing IVF,' she said. 'We just burned up thirty-one grand, but at least I don't have to fuck you.'

The two of them adopted the same tone of voice, one of conspicuous self-control, non-shouting. He said he didn't want to have a baby with someone who found him repulsive. She flinched and said that it was hard not to experience a little resentment when she'd had to coax him into doing what every other man in that waiting room seemed to be able to do; he said that it wasn't his fault that the hospital was set up for men who used porn; she said that she wished he could have looked at some porn ahead of time, having been warned, by her, that it was going to be present in the room, and that she wished the pride he took in being the last non-porn-contaminated American man could have been weighed against other considerations.

A day passed without conversation. Luke brushed his teeth at the kitchen sink to avoid standing beside Rita in the bathroom and weathering her refusal of eye contact. In bed, she donned her wax earplugs and face-mask and turned away from him, curled on her side. When his alarm went off in the morning, he rushed to work, even though he wasn't required to go to the office that day. He came home to find Rita seated at the butcherblock kitchen island, eating microwave popcorn. She addressed him as he took off his coat.

'I don't have the luxury of staying angry,' she said. 'I called Dr Licavoli. She doesn't think either of the embryos has much chance of making it to blastocyst. She said it's best if we start another round as soon as we can, in two weeks, when I have my period.'

'So we need to come up with the money now.'

She nodded. 'She said it might have been your sperm that fucked us but it might have been my eggs. That's why we need to hurry. I'm not getting any younger.'

They ordered takeout, shut themselves in the study, and devised entreaties, taking turns at the keyboard and gesturing with chopsticks at the document on the screen, like a screenwriting team. Her parents, like his, were divorced bohemians threatening to outlive their nest eggs, whose growth had been stunted by leftist lapses of faith in the financial system, investments in gold and ethical portfolios. Two of their four parents had romantic partners who discouraged them from giving money to their children, and the other two lacked the means. They were all potential lenders, in other words, not potential donors. But they needed to be massaged as if they were the latter, given the astronomical sums involved. The email drafts proposed interest rates and schedules of repayment. They promised access to any resulting grandchild so unfettered it was tantamount to custody; and they stated, in euphemistic but unambiguous terms, that principal and interest would be mailed in hard cash, undetectable to the IRS. ('We are very comfortable with large bills and padded envelopes, if you are.') No lawyers, no paper trail. In all likelihood, they would never own an apartment, not on this coastline. But they would be able to service their debts and save up for day care, if they managed to have a baby in the end. When they were done, Rita went into the bedroom and called her mother, and then two of her best friends. He could hear her crying through the wall.

Afterward, he paced the kitchen and read her the drafts they'd composed, and she nodded, her back against the fridge, her head cocked to one side. She said she'd already broached the subject of a loan with her mother, who seemed receptive.

'Good work,' he said.

'You too.' They embraced but avoided eye contact. This reminded him of cats. 'Say we get all the money,' she said. 'It's round two. How do we know there won't be another crisis in the porn room?'

'I'll take something in there. Something to distract me from the atmosphere.'

'You mean a toy? A magazine?'

He shrugged.

'You need to think about it,' she said. 'Because we need it to work. I never want to go through that suspense in the waiting area again. That was hell. I think it's going to be hard for you, because you're going to be under even more pressure this time. This is the last stand for the Rita–Luke baby. We're both going to feel it.'

He deliberated. 'If I'm being honest,' he said, 'what would be most helpful would be for you to film yourself on your phone. Just go into the bedroom, take off your clothes, and jerk off. Maybe you could say something to me while you do it, but only if you feel inspired. If I could have that to watch, that would be the closest thing to taking you in there.'

She winced. 'Interesting.'

'I'm sorry,' he said. 'It's just that I find porn disgusting, because I'm not used to it, and so, if you want something that's going to work –'

'I get it. I have zero libido right now, because of the meds. But I'll do it.'

'I know it's hard to get all the way there,' he said, 'when you're being asked to get yourself all the way there.'

She shrugged. 'I can do it.'

He averted his eyes in shame, and then looked at her to see what she was doing. She opened a cupboard and took down a mug decorated with a faded flag of the Faroe Islands, where they'd gone on their final vacation, two years ago, before they'd started to squirrel everything away. She studied the contents of a tin. 'We're out of green tea,' she said. 'Okay. I'm going to pee, and then I'm going to go do it. Just don't come in. It would make me self-conscious.'

He marveled at the strength of her compulsion to strike any task from her to-do list as quickly as possible. She had an obsessive, prideful self-discipline that he'd always found irritating and attractive. While she peed, he sat at the kitchen island, spinning in circles on his stool, and wondered if he should thank her, or if that would be cloying, like thanking somebody for sex. 'Break a leg,' he said, as she opened the bathroom door and crossed the kitchen. She lingered in the bedroom's door-frame. Neither of them spoke for a little while.

'I can figure out something else,' he continued. 'It's too shitty, asking you to make a porn. Next time, I won't be shocked by the pictures on the monitor. I think it'll be okay.'

'You don't say "make a porn",' she said. 'It's "make porn". I'm going to get it over with. If the video doesn't do it for you, you have to let me know, and I'll try again.'

He wondered if she would turn on the overhead light in the bedroom, or go with the reading lamps, for ambience. Would she be cold, when she stripped, and lay on the bed? Their landlord skimped on heat, and it was always colder in there than in the rest of the apartment. Would she be haunted by the things he'd said during the fight? Would she fake it, and worry that, as her husband, he would be able to tell? Was she angry at him, despite her disavowal of anger? If they failed to have a child, she might be angry at him for a long time. They waved goodbye, for some reason, before she slipped into the darkness with her phone and shut the door. ∎

TEREZA ČERVEŇOVÁ

ENGLAND'S OTHER ISLAND

Owen Hatherley

One of the clichés about the Isle of Wight is that it is England in microcosm, a miniaturised Olde England confined to another much smaller island that you can traverse in under an hour. Despite its proximity to the mainland – ferries from Southampton take around forty-five minutes – the island has long had an ambiguous status. It was only officially ceded to England by France in the thirteenth century, and until the 1990s, it had a governor, like a colonial or overseas territory.

My father's mother and her sisters were among the Londoners who decamped to the island in the post-war years. When my family visited them in the decades that followed, the feeling of time having stopped and gone backwards was palpable. In 1950, the writer and painter Barbara Jones described the island as a series of medieval villages so pickled in the nineteenth century that they were effectively Victorian. I've visited at least every summer since 2018, and though it has diversified and loosened up a little, the island can still feel like a place where the nineteenth century never quite ended, a Victorian summer utopia perpetually falling into dereliction and desuetude, its eroding cliffs permanently threatening to plunge the seaside resorts below into the sea.

'Micro' is a frequent prefix on the island. There is a model village at Godshill, and a miniature village of small thatched houses in the town of Shanklin. This microcosmic quality inspired Julian Barnes's *England, England*, a laboured satire on John Major's nostalgic late-Thatcherite era, in which a malevolent Murdochian media corporation purchases and transforms the island into a theme park microcosm of the mainland, geared towards American tourists disappointed at the depressing reality of actually existing England. One of the corporation's blue-sky thinkers summarises the island's 'offer' to his boss as follows:

> 'What's it got we can use? A little bit of everything, I'd say, yet at the same time nothing too mega. Nothing we can't dispense with if need be. So. One castle, rather nice: ramparts, gatehouse, keep, chapel. No moat, but we could bung one in easily enough. Next, one royal palace: Osborne House, as noted by Dr Max. Italianate. Opinions differ. Two resident monarchs: Charles the first, in captivity at the said castle before his execution; Queen Victoria, in residence at the said palace, where she died. Feature possibilities in either, I'd say. One resident famous poet: Tennyson . . . Many thatched cottages, perfect for tea-shops. Correction: most of which already are tea-shops, but suitable for upgrade . . .'
>
> 'Fill it in!' chortled Sir Jack. 'Concrete it over!'

A staggering procession of the great and the good spent their winters here in the second half of the nineteenth century. I have occasionally told myself that if I ever decided to make my fortune, I would write a *League of Extraordinary Gentlemen*-style work in which some of the various figures who were at one point resident here – Victoria, Marx, Darwin, Dickens, Tennyson, Julia Margaret Cameron, Garibaldi, Wilhelm II, Nicholas II – encounter each other and discuss politics and philosophy in a Shanklin Olde Village Tea Shoppe. What makes this litany of historic names surreal for anyone who knows the Isle of Wight is the place's decidedly ordinary character, so ordinary it comes out the other end into the actively weird.

The ordinariness owes a little to the changing patterns of residency on the island. The haute bourgeoisie and aristocracy who once patronised the place can seem, in towns like Ryde or Shanklin or Newport, to have abandoned it, but after 1945, the London working class and petite bourgeoisie flocked to the island as they left the capital and retired, turning the resort conurbation of Shanklin–Sandown into what was frequently described as 'Little London'. From the sixties on, the Greater London Council used to buy up houses in these towns to offer to retiring Londoners, a programme that is still maintained to this day by the Greater London Authority's Seaside and Country Homes scheme.

Listening to people speaking on buses and trains on the island, its character today is broadly proletarian, although you can, it transpires, find a few posher enclaves inland and in the yachting centre of Cowes. This working-class character extends to the seldom-discussed fact that the island was once – and to an extent still is – a major industrial centre. The yachts of Cowes have often been built in East Cowes itself, on the other side of the Medina estuary from the Royal Yachting Squadron. Skilled shipbuilding here diversified in the twentieth century into flying boats, military ships and, eventually, hovercraft, which were effectively invented at the Saunders-Roe works in East Cowes in the 1950s and put into mass production here in the subsequent decade. These superfast but energy-intensive boats were icons of the Wilsonian 'White Heat of Technology', lightweight, curved, almost pop art designs; aptly, a hovercraft service still operates regularly between Portsmouth and Ryde on the island, claiming to be the world's last timetabled passenger service still using hovercraft. This sort of semi-obsolete futurism feels as much part of the island's character as its parish churches and tea rooms. Less cutely, the expertise of East Cowes' skilled workers has continued to lend itself to military use – there is a massive BAE Systems factory on the town's outskirts.

How you see the island as a visitor depends greatly on your port of entry. Southampton ships go to Cowes; the ships from Lymington in the New Forest go to Yarmouth; and the Portsmouth ships depart for Ryde from Portsmouth Harbour railway station. Each area takes on some of the qualities of the port of embarkation, with Yarmouth and its surroundings resembling the New Forest, East Cowes and Newport's red-brick industrial streets approximating those of Southampton, and Ryde, acquiring some of Portsmouth's firmly proletarian naval aggression. This is the route I usually take.

The quintessentially English White Cliff that encircles the island is flanked to the south by the start of the Undercliff. Here, you could be not so much in the Riviera as somewhere in the South Pacific, a yellow, craggy, perpetually crumbling, subsiding wall with exotic trees growing out of and on top of it. Between these cliffs are several miles of beaches, the main attraction both for consumptive Victorian intellectuals and retired twentieth-century cockneys. It's here, in a guest house facing the beach in Shanklin, that my partner and I stay every year. I have stared at this bay for hours, pausing for fish and chips or games of *Space Invaders* in the arcades. Perhaps part of the appeal of this place for me, though, was inadvertently summed up by Pennethorne Hughes in his 1960s *Shell Guide* to the island: it 'rises so cheerfully from the bay that, despite having no architectural merit whatsoever, it is easy to call it beautiful'. That means, as an architectural writer, that I do not feel implored to do any work here.

The stretch between Ryde and Ventnor is the part I know best, a place to which I am – irrespective of its occasionally terrifyingly xenophobic politics – firmly and sentimentally attached. The other entry point to the island is different, and a place where it is much harder to screen out your bad thoughts. East Cowes was always just a blur of car parks and red-brick terraces. West Cowes, however, is the famous Cowes, home of the Cowes Regatta, an annual upper-class boat festival, and also the home of the Royal Yachting Squadron, which still has its own specialised Victorian cast iron pier, entered beneath an ornate lantern. The townscape is not dissimilar to that of

Ryde – early Victorian, so still with a certain Georgian grace and less of Shanklin and Sandown's gawky high-Victorian heaviness, with a lot of bay windows and a lot of verandas.

The gentle, sun-kissed melting together of melancholia and kiss-me-quick kitsch of the island I know was nowhere to be seen in Cowes in 2024. Rather than the enjoyable but faintly sad mix of tourist shops, junk shops, caffs and pubs-that-time-forgot that you find between Ryde and Ventnor, West Cowes's main shopping street is devoted to the sort of middle-class fine dining you find in south-west London or Surrey – gastropubs, 'Japanese fusion' restaurants, places selling very highly priced windcheaters. One shopfront has an opaque glass wall and, in small sans serif letters, OLESINSKI. SUPERYACHTS. The major cultural attraction is a freakish collection of eighteenth- and nineteenth-century nauticalia – paintings, model boats, figureheads – on the upper floor of a boat store, put together by one-time resident, yachter, Conservative MP and *Daily Express* proprietor, Max Aitken, son of the notorious Lord Beaverbrook.

Cowes gradually gives way to Newport, where all the things needed for a modern existence – general hospital, shopping mall, bus station, leisure centre, municipal offices – are clustered around a historic core still defined by a couple of surviving Nash civic buildings. People here look tired, worried and cheaply dressed, as they do in most English urban centres.

From the Victorians on, this island has, without anyone ever planning it, become a place where people have imagined their utopias, evanescent or permanent. Most of these have been personal utopias, holiday homes you would never have to leave, in a place where summer would never have to end – but there are two exceptions, two major works of architecture and landscape where a way of life has been worked out with considerable thought. Osborne and Quarr are the only two buildings that a serious architectural historian could seriously recommend on the island – though an *unserious* one would point out that there's a lot else to look at. Osborne is the Italianate

'House' that Victoria and Albert built for themselves in the 1840s – their own Peterhof, or bonsai Versailles. It is a disturbing vision of personal luxury directly overlooking the sources of that wealth: a bronze statue of a bound slave girl on the terrace gazes out over an estuary from which the ships would have sailed to countless dirty wars in China, New Zealand, South Africa and elsewhere.

The other utopia overlooking the busy shipping lane is considerably more communal. Quarr Abbey was founded by French Cistercian monks in the twelfth century and destroyed under Henry VIII a few hundred years later. The French monks returned at the start of the twentieth century – fleeing the Third Republic's secularising reforms – one of whom, Dom Paul Bellot, doubled as an architect. He designed a series of remarkable abbeys and churches in the Dutch Expressionist style; intricately constructed from red brick, placed into strange, quasi-Gothic, organic shapes: a path from nineteenth-century medievalism into an architecture of pure space and fearless form. Its austerity – hardly any sculpture, no paintings, only the most minimal stained glass – is combined with a richness of light, shafts of which emphasise the rugged arches. The bricks were imported from Flanders, but the workers were not – Quarr was built by the exact same island masons who were at the time erecting the indifferent Edwardian suburban semis and guest houses that spread around the edges of the island's towns. They *could* build works like this, but that was never going to make a profit. ■

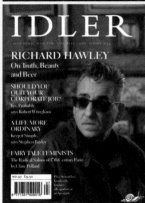

AN ORDINARY ISLE

Photography by Tereza Červeňová

JERWOOD PHOTOGRAPHY COMMISSIONS

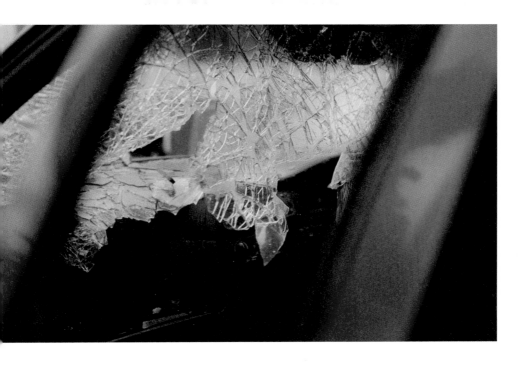

Get on board with **Bookworm** for your *free* weekly dose of exclusive reviews, book excerpts, and much more.

Visit *reviewcanada.ca/streetcar* or scan the code below.

Literary Review of Canada

A JOURNAL OF IDEAS

LEWIS KHAN
Theatre, 2020

APPENDIX

K Patrick

An hour before surgery Dr Duncan ducked into the men's bathroom. The women's was another twenty-minute walk away and usually, on this side of the hospital, the bathroom was empty. But there was Ian, a surgical resident, posed against the grotty sinks. His phone lifted above his head, angled down, one hand moving beneath the blue of his scrubs. The moment he saw her, he stopped. A statue. But he did not withdraw his hand. The shape of his fingers flattened as he launched into an apology.

It's just a photo, he spoke softly. It's just a photo, honestly.

I shouldn't have been in here, Dr Duncan replied. It's fine.

Still he did not withdraw his hand. He put his phone beside the sink, screen down. Unhygienic, she thought, looking at the phone, imagining the dirty glass pressed to his ear. The bathroom's details were otherwise familiar. She knew which cubicle had the cracked toilet seat, which tap ran viciously hot. Before he could say anything else she stepped back into the corridor.

Had things gone differently, Dr Duncan would have let Ian take the lead on the appendectomy. He'd have had the opportunity to gently push the tube, containing the light and camera, through the opened belly button and watch the inching of the large intestine as it appeared on the screen. Instead she would perform the first cut.

Skin prised underneath the blade. The camera sunk in. She would have remarked, had Ian been holding the scalpel, that the large intestine was like a sea monster, mythical, moved along by its own pink pulse. She would have shaken her head and expressed her awe at the human body, asked him to consider that he might be the only person to ever see this part of the patient, that it was important not to let the significance of that intimacy pass you by. But Dr Duncan had changed her mind.

Ian paused, seemingly unfazed, beside the operating table. His hands in blue latex gloves. He did everything handsomely. He was gay, very gay, in his own words, and the other female residents flocked to him, knowing they wanted a piece of the ancient light that bounced off his body.

At Dr Duncan's command, Ian dutifully took the disposal razor and tried to shave the top rows of the patient's pubic hair. He struggled to find the right angle, twisting his elbows this way and that, dragging too lightly across the tough hairs, then too hard, threatening to nick the skin. One of the nurses flinched. When it was done, the low boil of a rash left behind, he did not look at Dr Duncan. He focused on the screen that showed the camera's worming journey.

This would be the last operation of Dr Duncan's shift. Later she would collect her son from the airport. He'd chosen a cheap flight, one that landed just before midnight. She had not seen him in a few months. Alex, who had grown up to be tall and broad, who was also handsome.

As the camera advanced through the bowel, she hummed quietly, a kind of theme tune. Alex had got into a decent university, if a little far away, and at eighteen was now old enough that they indulged in similar tastes; he claimed to like red wine, which he swished and swilled, named music she remembered from when she was his age. He'd told her, on his last visit, that he and his friends had drunk the bottle she'd sent to him out of stained mugs, knowing it might rile her. She resisted. Well, as long as you enjoyed it. Oh, we did, he said, insinuating what was just out of shot, the part of the picture she couldn't see.

Through the belly button she filled the patient's abdomen with gas, pushing out the walls of the large intestine, making it easier to navigate the sluggish turns. After that came the camera and the private, fleshy undertones, the surfaces slick and shining.

The appendix appeared. Half of it already distended, deep maroon, a twisted and flashing smile. Dr Duncan was satisfied. She had been right. The patient, who had arrived yesterday evening, complaining of pain in her right-hand side, no fever but an elevated white blood cell count, had been suffering from appendicitis. Now it had been caught before a perforation. She announced this to Ian, asked him to look at the appendix, veins drifting thin as hair, the bloated glow. He nodded over her shoulder. Briefly her elbow made contact with his chest.

The patient had tattoos. Not only down her arms but, as Dr Duncan looked back at her body from the screen, along the tops of her thighs. One was a quote in cursive that was too difficult to read upside down, then a giant flower, maybe a magnolia, that bloomed all the way to her knee. There was a smaller scene, birds across a sunset, a boat, the whole thing very elaborate.

Dr Duncan had her own tattoo. In black ink along her ribs, on the left-hand side. It was Alex's full name, Alexander, done when he was already twelve years old. She'd practised writing it out beforehand, wanted it in lower case, lengthening the first 'e' so it would not be immediately recognisable as his, adding a flourish to the 'r'. A literal impulse, she knew. Her body was already marked by his birth, the scar of the C-section faint but still visible across her stomach. It was around the time that the name she'd given him had begun to permanently change, his loud friends calling him Al, or, inexplicably, X. Her ex-husband, too, who had never said Alexander. Right from the beginning, he had always used Alex. These were the names her son chose to have on his homework, the signatures he gave on her birthday cards.

At the parlour, sitting on an old leather sofa, she'd been asked about placement. The tattoo artist listed body parts with bizarre distortions, inside finger, soft bit of forearm, lower-back dip, upper-back spine, pelvic gutter. Just somewhere it won't be seen, she'd stated. He'd twisted then, pointed to his own ribcage. Yes, there.

Dr Duncan clamped and quickly clipped the appendix free. It was then scooped out in a small wire basket, which, despite the meticulously tried and tested design, always made Dr Duncan think of catching fish in a deep-fat fryer. At the incision's entrance, she repositioned and slowly pulled the appendix through. The patient's skin puckered, beastly, glorious, protesting with an organised spill of blood.

Hey presto, she said aloud.

Ian smiled too large behind his mask, she saw the lift of his eyes, thrilled by a catchphrase that barely belonged to her.

The whole idea, she added quickly, was of course to avoid perforation while it was still inside the body, thus the basket, thus the swift and gentle exit.

Thus, Ian echoed, hey presto.

Dr Duncan did not advance. She let the appendix hover over the patient's body. In Ian's tone she'd heard the arrogance of a private joke, where no joke had been shared. He stood, hands outstretched and empty. She took another few seconds. Brought the appendix close to her face. Saw again confirmation that her instincts were good, that she'd been right to operate. She pinched it and felt the leathery resistance of the infected end. The other half was still bright, spongy. Another couple of days though, even one more day, and it might have burst.

She passed it on to Ian, who stepped away. Set the appendix in a metal bowl. A nurse collected it. From this moment on it would become a specimen, sent to the hospital lab for a few further tests, which would most likely reveal nothing they couldn't already see.

On the way to the airport she would need to stop at the supermarket. Dr Duncan wondered whether she should buy the body wash her son liked. Last time she'd noticed, when she'd gone into the bathroom after he'd used it, a strong minty smell that carried on the residual steam. He'd brought with him small, travel-size containers, a brand she didn't recognise at first but had since seen in a pharmacy, on the shelves of the supermarket. Maybe he used something different, now. That had been two, no, three months ago.

The small opening in the large intestine was stapled shut. Gas was released from the patient's abdomen. Later she might experience a pain both sharp and blunt between her shoulder blades, as if she had been flicked and the flick had held, as a few escaped bubbles travelled north. The patient, hopefully, would have only one night in hospital before being discharged. There had been an anomaly, blood in her urine, but this could be an oncoming period, unrelated to the appendicitis. On admission the patient could not remember where she was in her cycle. Mid? she'd replied, eyebrows raised, as if this was something Dr Duncan could confirm.

She allowed Ian to stitch the incision across the abdomen. She pointed at the opened belly button, the smaller, second incision to the left.

Do those too, and do them well.

He nodded, his eyes on the abdomen.

Yes?

Yes, I'll do them.

Alex saw her tattoo when he was thirteen, a year or so after she'd had it done. They were on a beach holiday and she'd opted to wear a bikini. It was just the two of them, her divorce already under way and her ex-husband living moodily in a new city. She waited, that first day in the sun, for Alex to ask what was written beneath her armpit. He stalked the shoreline, crouching to sort through shells, his legs and ankles thick with those interim years, his body not yet ascended into the muscle and stretch of teenagedom. He glanced at her tattoo, or at least she thought he had, but said nothing. She became bolder, turned, angled her left-hand side so it faced him. Still nothing. He was a private child and it seemed he'd given her this in return, a privacy, whether she wanted it or not. She supposed, applying suncream to the backs of his legs, his neck, the tops of his ears, the places he forgot, that this was being a mother.

The nurses wheeled the patient into the recovery bay. Many patients, as they saw Dr Duncan standing over their bodies, the pain of which they could not yet feel, would sob softly. She knew that this was for various, impersonal reasons. Namely the thinning out of the general anaesthetic, the patients arriving back into the world on a foreign, tidal pull. They would remember nothing of the interaction afterwards.

As the patient's eyelids bobbed, the eyeballs searching underneath the delicate skin, Dr Duncan stood beside her and waited. The patient's hair was short, curly, shaved beside the ears. As she opened her eyes Dr Duncan could see the surgery's effect, her pupils lost to its heavy weather. Sure enough the patient began to sob silently, to reject the tube in her throat. Her hand, the cannula tugging in her forearm, moved to find Dr Duncan, who squeezed her palm.

It's all fine, everything is fine, it went very well indeed.

The patient nodded. Fell back to sleep.

Another mother – was it her own? – said to her that you knew a child's body best in illness. It was true enough. When he was six, Alex had two bouts of pneumonia. In bed for a month, then more. She intuited when he was lying on his back from the distant wheeze in his exhale. If he was lying on his front, the note would shift into a whistle. A long, boneless breath meant he could not easily be woken, that his fever remained at a peak. She could recall the scatter of his room, toys boxed in by other toys, arranged in concentric audiences, just as he'd left them before he was ill. She never tidied them away. The bears watched the toy soldiers who watched the race cars who watched the marbles. There was the pretty way Alex looked at her, too, eyes glassy, his hair spread neat and still against the pillow. As an adult he claimed not to remember any of it. She'd tried to prompt him. Mentioned the splendid delirium of his dreams. That when she'd soothed him he'd press into her neck and offer solitary, wandering words. Rhubarb, otter, flute. He'd only shake his head. Sorry, guess I was pretty out of it! Key, grass, hat.

Ian watched Dr Duncan reassure the patient. The way he leaned into the door frame, his hip tilted, arms folded, indicated that it was she, Dr Duncan, who might have something to learn. To leave the room she had to walk right up to him, see his arms fall back to his sides, palms wiped briefly on his thighs. He moved with her into the corridor. An urgency in his proximity. He spoke too close to her ear.

That all went smoothly, didn't it?

What do you think?

Her authority was lessened, she felt, by the way her shoes squeaked against the pale green linoleum. She did not want his apology. It was building in him, she could feel it, that terrible crescendo. Twice he inhaled deeply. Twice he released the sigh through his nose, sounding all the dramatic tones of a poorly played instrument. Nothing had to be acknowledged. In this, the aftermath, they ought to dim the bathroom's unforgiving brightness, let the scene, the slow movement of his hand, recede into whatever darkness. Time would take care of things. When it came to the next appendectomy she would likely let him make the first cut.

She kept on walking, though was no longer sure where she should walk to. She was concerned Ian might place his hand on her shoulder. He kept pace, watching his feet, or listening to hers.

The first or second day of his residency she found Ian's eyes washed up on her collarbone. He watched the movement of her two necklaces, how they'd entwined, seeking out the disc the size of a thumbprint, St Christopher hunched over and on his sanctified way. Later, when she'd removed her jewellery for a gallbladder procedure, Ian had watched again, this time following her fingers as she'd worked the two clasps, then dropped the necklaces into the small dish.

Was there anything else?

No, no. Ian retreated.

Dr Duncan slipped into a nurses' station. Brewed a coffee. Ran through the meals she had made Alex on his last visit. On the final night she'd cooked a chicken chasseur, a dish she'd recently learned. It had never occurred to her to take apart a whole chicken, to lever the knife through the joints, slide out the breasts. Alex wandered into the kitchen. Mum, Jesus, that's a bit intense. Still, he'd stood and watched, impressed, unable to fight his own fascination. Once she finished the job, her hands washed, she turned to face him. He was holding his breath tightly. It was a child's habit, the lesson learned early on, an attempt to pause fear, to force the chest steady. Between them was an anticipatory silence, the rock before it hits the water. She waited. He certified some unknown feature of her gaze. Said absolutely nothing where there was something. He gave up their moment quickly, breaking it with a yawn, a faux stretch. He pointed at her new and enormous knife. Fucking hell, so when did you buy that?

She checked the clock above the sink. The surgery had been faster than scheduled. Alex would be at the airport waiting to board. He did like to send a message, to let her know that it was all on time, add the crossed-fingers emoji, sometimes a blue heart. The university was not so far away. If he'd learned to drive then he could have covered the distance by car. But he'd shown no interest, none of the usual boyish and chaotic excitement that she had seen in his schoolmates. When she'd pushed, explained that it wasn't so hard, that he should really get on with it, his lack of interest had become a kind of protest.

Dr Duncan had taken the next day off. She would not be around to, if all went well overnight, discharge the patient herself. She wanted some time with Alex. Had not told him though, it occurred to her now, and he might have made other plans. There were still a couple of school friends that hadn't yet gone to university, working instead, saving money to travel. There was a moment when Alex might have done the same. A couple of years ago he kept a world map preciously on his bedroom wall. Made his own key, a star for where he definitely wanted to go, a circle for a maybe. Dotted lines showed flight paths, a few costs had even been labelled. But then his plan had changed with no explanation, the whole map ripped down. Not thrown away, she'd noticed, but folded and slid underneath his bed.

She decided on a lasagne. An old dish, the kind of thing she'd batch-cooked when Alex was still a pre-teen, enjoyed a little fame for it, his friends requesting it when they came to stay. They could eat it tomorrow night. She'd already ordered some decent red wine online, planned to put his palate to the test, and he'd roll his eyes but be quietly pleased.

Her office was small and virtually pointless. She was almost never in it. But she took a moment now to check her phone. Sipped her coffee. Yes, Alex had sent two messages, All on time! Followed by his blue heart. She replied with a thumbs up. She ought to write a shopping list, knew the way her mind could slip once she left the hospital.

A gentle knocking. Ian spoke into the crack in the door, not showing his face.

Do you have a minute?

Exactly one.

So it would have to happen, this apology. He did not enter the room immediately. She imagined he rehearsed his lines again, a phraseology second-guessed and adjusted.

Are you coming in?

He closed the door gently. Please, she wanted to scream, dear God, don't create an atmosphere. The office was ugly. There were no paintings on the walls, not a photo in sight.

How can I help?

I just wanted to say that before, he cleared his throat, with what happened before, I don't want you to get the wrong idea, those photos, they were just for my boyfriend, that's all, it's just a bit of fun.

There was a benefit, at least, to being the bearer of forgiveness. In the long beat of an apology, there is a luxury of seconds, a surplus, permission to really look at a person. The expert melancholia in his eyes. His skin very clear, his nails very short, a nice shape. A scar, like a white comma, across the knuckle of his pinky finger.

Please. She held up her hand. It's fine, like I said before, I shouldn't have been in the men's. She leaned forward for effect. I should say though, while we're here, that it's just important to be professional. That's all I ask, for you to conduct yourself in a certain way. Don't get upset, it's just part of the job, an easy part if you'd just let it be easy.

He sucked in his cheeks.

I do, I do see.

Good, that's all I ask.

She pretended to dial a number. Nodded. Waved him back out of the door.

Dr Duncan wondered if it was true, whether Ian really had sent the picture to his boyfriend, if he even had only one boyfriend. And whoever it was for, what was understood about the image, then, once it was received, once it had left the hospital's apparently irresistible space and travelled elsewhere, into a different room, a different building entirely. The body translated and re-translated, then well used by somebody else. It was a favour, she guessed, that would have to be returned. Ian had held the phone above his head so carefully, lifted his chin precisely to the right, left room for the flat of his stomach, the bulge of his crotch, the landscape of his fist visible through the thin cotton. She could've counted the knuckles.

Dr Duncan and Ian were not close, but at fifty-seven, her gender, the fact she was a woman surgeon, had meant interest in her life where there had been none before. It was a temperamental currency but she was happy to engage, to say yes when invited to speak, to nod in empathetic agreement that it must have been terribly hard.

Ian's fixation was Dr Duncan's time in Strasbourg. She told him she'd been the only woman studying and specialising in laparoscopic procedures at the university there, although it wasn't the truth. There had been at least two, no, three other women she could remember. She recalled his wide expression, her fingers on her St Christopher pendant as he listened, asked questions. The conversation had delighted him. He wanted to travel, he spoke to the history of laparoscopy, pointed out the obvious, that it was not one man that had invented, or even pioneered the concept, but a series of separate nineteenth-century surgeons who had all landed on the same thought, across different continents. When Ian said 'man' he added air quotations, not to doubt their maleness, she gathered, but to acknowledge the deficit. It was always the daring predictability of the human body that enamoured him, he'd added, wanting to impress her, that these 'men' would individually come to the same conclusion, that the appendix would be found at the end of the large intestine. Yes, she'd agreed. Suspended as a lone piece of grammar. He'd liked that.

When it came to words, her ex-husband had been no good. Every thought of him she resisted, the eye of her memory half shut. There was one that broke through with irritating regularity. A fight, only medium-sized, and him with a small towel wrapped around his thickened waist. The sentences that left his mouth. He stood damp and stupid in the corner of their old bedroom. Hence, he shouted. Thus, therefore, ergo. Periphrastic, she should have accused.

There was nothing left to sign. Thankfully no new emergency admissions that needed her. Dr Duncan locked her office door. Normally, she'd throw on jeans, boots, leave on her clean scrub top. Maybe a jumper. But this time she wanted a gentle difference, to look a little less like his mother. Her mascara was clumpy, old and barely used, but she applied it in persuasive strokes. Lipstick on, then removed, it was too much. There was, as it turned out, a line. Hair down, brushed, she sprayed through dry shampoo and hated, really hated, the sweet smell. She went to switch out her jewellery and then stopped.

She sat back at her desk. There really was nothing in the room to look at. She didn't know if the other surgeons, those with offices, bothered with pictures. Perhaps an ailing plant. Ian had stood there and seen nothing else of her. Only a torso, her face and neck. The St Christopher, which he already knew.

She took out her phone. Typed gay porn into the search bar. Chose the first website, with its promise of FREE and SKILLED MOUTHS. She scrolled down the page, each video on offer played briefly, the highlights, she supposed, as her thumb slid over the screen. One after another. Volume up, then down. SEXY STUDS squatted on a blue carpet. An open car door, a man bent over another man's lap, a third man in the passenger seat. Denim was unbuttoned, hard cocks revealed. No underwear, she noted. There was a state of readiness. A kiss with an apocalyptic urgency. In an empty gym, they knelt, sucked, eyes not closed but opened. Moved like winners. She had expected something else but didn't know what.

In the women's bathroom she pumped pink soap into her hands. She leaned closer to the mirror. Decided she looked nice, the mascara was worth it. But the lipstick had not been properly removed, caught in the cracks. She rubbed her mouth with the back of her hand.

A few bits of paperwork to sign and then she could leave. She walked out of the hospital, unlocked her car and sat in the driver's seat. She always took exactly a minute, hands placed on the wheel, without turning on the engine. It wasn't a ritual so much as a reckoning with the world, the one that existed separately to the hospital's surging and specific reality. It was the light. Tonight, her vision smoky with fatigue, it was a navy blue, full of shadows and gaps, almost everything reduced to its simplest shape. There was a time, during her first months as a general surgeon, when she found it hard to reconcile, to decide which was truer, the hospital or the rest, whatever came after. Now she knew it didn't matter. It was only the light. Her retinas adjusting, contracting.

Alex had taken a similar flight last time, landing late. Once again she would be picking him up after a long shift. When she was younger she'd woken up to the sound of traffic cones hitting her bumper, having briefly fallen asleep at the wheel. She didn't sleep well. Alex had been an insomniac toddler, in need of company. He'd quietly enter their bedroom, wake her up by placing his cold hands on her cheeks. For a few years, too many years maybe, she'd made up a single mattress for him on the floor beside her.

She started the engine. Would skip the supermarket for tonight. There'd be a chance to go first thing, before he was up, breakfast would be ready before he'd even realised she had gone.

It was expensive to park at the airport and so she'd instructed him to wait by the kerb. She spotted him easily. His lovely shoulders in a nice shirt, a new jacket, both black and stylish. She saw, too, that he was talking to somebody, laughing into his phone. He spotted her seconds later, waving, hanging up as he did so. She did not ask, once he'd settled into the passenger seat, who it had been and he did not offer the information either. An ellipsis strung between them. A slight and shifting tension, elbow to elbow.

She asked ordinary questions.

How was the flight, had he eaten, what were his plans, how was his course, did he have enough money?

He answered fully. Kept his phone in his pocket. She heard it vibrate.

They picked up a pizza. He was tired, happy to eat in front of the TV. Later, when he'd fallen asleep on the sofa, she picked it up and tried to guess his passcode. Not his birthday, not her birthday. He slept on, his lips pursed, the way he looked as a child, his hands slid down his trackpants to grip his knees. It was a decision as obvious as her tattoo. Not a sense of ownership but an impulse, fragile, that deserved to be acted on. There was no futurity, what she expected to find, and then what she might feel as a consequence. She'd tried his father's birthday, not that either. There had been no pets in the family, no short and beloved names she could try and translate into the numeric. He stirred, repositioned his body. She stood beside him. The phone glowed in her hand.

Alex's screen saver was a pile of small, pinkish shells on a wooden surface, either a dining table or a windowsill. The image was zoomed in, his fingers dragged across the screen to enlarge what he'd noticed. It meant nothing to her. A shaft of light fell across the centre of the pile, turning those shells pinker. She supposed Alex had found the moment beautiful, enough that he wanted to look at it every day, every few minutes, however often he lifted his phone to his face.

As if she had caught its scent, Dr Duncan thought of the second house she had bought with her ex-husband. It had been her favourite. A purchase made on certain romantic whims. The complication of wisteria, untended for decades, across the arched, single-glazed windows. A large pond in the back garden, supposedly made by seventeenth-century monks, surrounded by rare varieties of self-seeded mint that had once been planted in a kind of holy herb garden.

Out the back of the house, over a wall, was a field, also theirs. At the closest end was a large, grassy mound. A burial cairn, empty after raids over the ensuing centuries, of which they were now the official guardians.

Alex, too, had loved that house. He'd just turned nine. Together they bullied her ex-husband into taking it on. He was put off by old buildings, thanks to childhood summers spent in a great aunt's collapsing cottage, where he'd placed a Bible beneath his pillow, believing it would ward off any evil as he slept.

Alex made a brief friend at his new school. A boy with a laugh that came out of nowhere, it made her jump, leaving such quiet in its wake. For a month or so the boy would come over every other day, staying for dinner, the pair of them obsessed with treasure. Thrilled to find a small blue apothecary bottle beneath a floorboard, a possible arrowhead in the garden. Their archive collected on a kitchen windowsill, where it had stayed, even after the friendship had ended. Together they kneeled over portions of earth and dug ferociously. Celebrating, high-fiving, grabbing each other's shoulders over broken bits of clay pipe, shards of pottery, shapely stones.

That summer, from her bedroom window, she watched them poised on the mound, the burial cairn, lying on their stomachs, positioning and repositioning their shattered objects. Alex took on the boy's laugh, getting louder, and they then laughed into each other, heavily, sides colliding. Reached across lower backs to move things this way and that. There was a secret formula, a pattern they wanted to achieve. They liked, if it was the weekend and could wait out the dusk, to turn over onto their backs and lie underneath the fading orange sunset. And she'd let them. ■

THE MAGAZINE OF CHATHAM HOUSE. BRINGING GLOBAL AFFAIRS TO LIFE SINCE 1945

MAEN HAMMAD
From *Landing*, Palestine, 2019

TROUBADOUR

Edward Salem

A bu Hammam was the best kind of hole in the wall. Low ceilings, dirty linoleum floors, and perfectly cooked mensef, my favorite meal. A chaos of male voices greeted you as you walked in, coming from harried waiters and bronze-dark men in white smocks shouting over fryers and burbling pots, but I never felt uncomfortable eating there alone as a woman. You'd figure out on your own that you had to go upstairs if you wanted a seat, turning the corner on the landing into the quieter, lower-ceilinged room with plastic chairs and tables lined against the dingy walls, a few crooked pictures of the Dome of the Rock and the Kaaba hanging above them. Anything you ordered came with a hot stack of fluffy pita bread, which I never ate but took home for the birds, spreading crumbs around the soil near my olive trees.

When I first heard the restaurant's name, I thought it meant Father of the Bathroom. Abu, father; hammam, bathroom – the only difference between the last name Hammam and the word for bathroom being a hard and soft H, a detail that was almost indiscernible to my immigrant ears. I only spoke Arabic when I visited Palestine and I'd lose a lot of the language in between visits. Abu Hammam referred, of course, to the family name, perhaps even a distant wing of my own extended family, the Hamamehs, who lived in McMansions in Texas and the outskirts of my village, Jiljilyya.

Hamameh, incidentally, sounded equally to my ears like the word for pigeon, a euphemism for penis.

I ate mensef at Abu Hammam once a week, often alone but sometimes with Wadiyeh, who still hadn't returned the case of DVDs I'd lent her on my previous trip to Palestine. Wadiyeh was an aspiring filmmaker who produced short interviews for an under-watched Ramallah news program. She was twenty-six, drank and smoked too much, and led men on, but I'm pretty sure she was still a virgin. She wore tight jeans and nude-colored heels, and when she leaned in to gossip or remark on a woman's bad fashion, I could smell the powdery makeup she'd smoothed across her jawline like an airbrushed Lebanese TV presenter. I'd first met Wadiyeh at Beit Aneeseh, and soon we were sharing an argileh without wiping the nozzle, passing it lip to lip, pulling and exhaling minty vaporous smoke in the dimly lit garden of the historic single-story limestone house that served as the bar. At almost every table I saw people sharing the argileh nozzle, one passing it to the next with a cursory wipe.

It was Wadiyeh who'd invited me to the quasi-underground, loosely kept secret that was the monthly queer party for out and less out Palestinians hosted at some apartment, often one near the gouged-out construction site where Salam Fayyad's people parked their cranes and bulldozers, or a big 1950s-era walk-up at the end of a street of newish, white limestone five-story buildings. I went every month, even though there were always too many white activists and upper-class European NGO workers, foreign queers and queer adjacents who were there for the anecdote, hoping to bed a native before their visa ended. This wasn't really a problem, since Palestinians liked fucking foreigners just as much; it was easier being with people who wouldn't be around for more than a few months or a year.

An hour into the party, both of us already drunk, Wadiyeh tried dragging me to some straight white guy's apartment to drink and have a *Monty Python* marathon with a small breakaway group. I took her hand off my shoulder and flinched at her beer breath. I slurred that I was here to find someone to actually fuck, not play games with. She stared at me, taking in this breach of our friendship, but said nothing. She was too invested in her social standing to be seen spatting and left with the white guy and his group. I wasn't sure if I meant what I said or if I just wanted to antagonize her, but when I thought about it, I decided I did mean it.

I scanned the room of frumpy couches, a makeshift dance floor and scruffy, curly-haired men dancing or absorbed in conversation. Almost everyone wore black T-shirts, which bored me, smoked and guffawed and tossed their curly hair, which bored me, and it was impossible to tell who was gay or straight, though everyone gave off straight vibes, which bored me. The Palestinian women all seemed cliquish, but I struck up conversation with a few and they were warm enough, if poised and too well mannered. One of them was supposedly Ghada Karmi's daughter. She spoke with a very proper British accent and gave off super, super straight vibes. I wasn't sure what she was doing there. Maybe she was into the novelty. I had my eyes on a woman I learned was from Haifa, with a buzz cut and maroon chandelier earrings and a black PFLP T-shirt, which suggested she would only be into other people who lived and breathed activism, wore black T-shirts and presented less femme than I did, even though I wasn't that femme. But I was annoyed with myself for being most attracted to a Spaniard, Lucía, whom I'd met once or twice at daytime political rallies I happened upon at the Manara Square. She brought me over a glass of cheap white wine when she noticed mine was empty.

Lucía had mascara-framed hazel eyes and wavy caramel hair, and was wearing a red spaghetti-strap tank top and baggy jeans that hung loosely from her hips. There was a sprig of hair at her belly button. We sat on a cracked leather couch, drinking and sharing spit on her cigarette, when a small group of brawny Palestinian dykes walked in. They wore oversized T-shirts and shorts with high-top sneakers and had their hair bunched into tight buns or tucked under backwards-facing baseball caps. I couldn't work out who was with whom based on where they sat, and Lucía and I played mix and match trying to work it out. Lucía said she had a long-term, long-distance girlfriend who wouldn't leave her job in Madrid to join her in Palestine. She said they were 'mostly open', but seemed to be stretching the truth, and when I pressed, she admitted that the girlfriend hadn't fully come around to the idea yet. I didn't want to get involved in anything complicated, so I made an excuse and called a cab home.

A t home in bed, I turned the brightness down on my phone and went through my nightly ritual of mindlessly checking the apps. I was surprised to see Rohit on offer again. I'd rejected her once, but through a glitch in the algorithm, she was back on my screen. I swiped through her pics and paused again on the one I'd paused on last time – her posing in a pale pink dress with one hand on the trunk of an olive tree wrapped in white string lights. I pinched my thumb and forefinger on her face like forceps and zoomed in. The name Rohit didn't fit her. Just as Netanyahu was born Mileikowsky in Philadelphia, Rohit might've been a Kristen or Courtney in the suburbs of Detroit. Her name was an obvious attempt at Fertile Crescent indigenization, but it sounded more like an Indian man's name, not a white girl's.

Her profile said she was Middle Eastern and liberal, which made me laugh. She was a vegetarian open to either monogamy or non-monogamy. She didn't have kids but might want them someday. Under the 'I could probably beat you at' question, where people typically wrote answers like baking or Call of Duty or movie trivia, Rohit wrote, 'I could probably just beat you.'

I swiped to the next photo – she was lying on large rocks in full military uniform, her dark blonde hair tossed across the ground, a rifle resting diagonally across her chest. On a whim I swiped right and my screen flashed with the silhouette of a five-pointed star saying we'd matched. I was perplexed. I figured she was the type to swipe left on Palestinians just as I was the type to reject Israelis.

I went back to the photo of her in uniform and noticed she wore a thumb ring and had painted her nails white, which matched the

Hebrew letters emblazoned on her black bulletproof vest. The next picture was off-center, Rohit sticking out her pointy tongue next to a crooked fragment of snow-covered trees. I wondered where she was, what country the picture had been taken in. That could have been my opening question, I thought. But I was never going to message her. I blew my nose and tossed the tissue across my bed. I had no interest in meeting her, and yet I took screenshots of most of her pictures. There was something degrading about saving the pictures I enjoyed. I set my phone on the nightstand near my head, where the screenshots might slither into my subconscious while I slept.

I had nothing to do the next day. I didn't want to see Wadiyeh and own up to my shitty comment at the party, but I didn't want to stay home either, so I drove to West Jerusalem to bathe in eye contact with people who hate my kind. To pass by random Rohits on the street and make them avert their gaze. I peered through the glass walls of clothing boutiques populated by Eastern European women with scalded skin, then walked down the street and played my repugnant but titillating game, pulling my mouth into that lipless smile reserved for strangers. I nodded unrequitedly to Israeli men and women who saw my Arab face and turned from it. If I intuited that it was relatively safe, that they wouldn't lunge at me for a fistful of hair, I'd touch my tongue to the roof of my mouth twice to say 'Ahlan', *Welcome*, but meekly, so they couldn't be sure if it was meant for them. If I was braver and said it louder, more directly and looking right at them, it'd receive a harsh glare or an epithet muttered to my back, which gave me a little thrill up my spine. The nastier the look, the more guttural their insult, the harder I'd giggle as I walked past them.

'Don't Speak' played on a cafe's tinny speakers near the park bench where I sat and uncapped my Thermos of arak, ice cubes hurtling forward as I tipped the rim to my lips and swigged the cold cloudy drink. I loosely hummed along to Gwen Stefani, wishing I had the guts to break out in song and bother the people on the street, like the hunched man in my neighborhood in Detroit who walked with a cane, wearing knock-off Oakleys and bulky headphones as he belted the lyrics to hard rock songs only he could hear.

I was starting to get a little buzzed from the arak, savoring the milky anise flavor and gaining the courage to hum louder in the sunlight surrounded by these people who despised me. I raised my voice and searched for someone's stare to hold, but no one took the bait. They walked off like they were holding in a shit. I rose from the bench and walked back to my car, humming just loud enough to embarrass myself, provoking a few scowls from Israelis. My head swam and I heard the clink of the ice cubes jostling against the metal walls of the Thermos. I rode my nervous energy, singing quietly in Arabic now, but loudly enough to catch the attention of an elderly Orthodox couple with shopping bags sagging from their arms.

'Lau samaht, atwaslak,' I belted mockingly, staring at the man's averted eyes, cracking myself up as I pulled my car door open and slid in, flooded with nerves as I started the engine.

My phone vibrated on the glass coffee table and woke me from my nap. I'd dreamt I was picking the cancer out of my mother's open lungs like hornets from a nest, tossing the scraps to the side as if to a dog. Parched, I reached for the Thermos and regretted it, not prepared for the lukewarm, watered-down arak.

The house was miserably hot. The AC had cut out. I checked the thermostat, groggily jabbing the buttons, prying at the plastic cover until it creaked and snapped open. I replaced the batteries, expecting a hush of cool air, but nothing happened. My mind went to tampering – petty psychological warfare. I suspected they kept tabs on me, recording me from a distance. I felt it. They knew how much money I had, who I emailed and texted, where I went. That's what they got off on. I went to the kitchen to see if the electricity was on in the rest of the house and didn't see the green digital time on the stove. The fridge wasn't humming, and when I plugged my phone in, the icon in the top corner showed that it wasn't charging. So it was a simple power outage. The electricity would probably be out for hours.

Wadiyeh had texted me. I still didn't want to see her. I opened all the windows and changed into a tank top and sweat shorts, deciding against pulling the curtains shut, even if it meant the satellite cameras could capture my body. I didn't think administrative assistants in military uniform were staring at me on a monitor in real time, or an incel soldier was spitting in his hand in an empty control room, just that it was all uploaded onto a hard drive in the basement of some temperature-controlled government facility. An archive of digital videos of me cooking and putzing, going inside to refill my tea and get a snack, fingering my cellphone on the chair out back.

Sitting on the warm, sunlit couch cushions in plain view of the open window, I brought out my poppers and shook the vial to disturb the tiny white pellet within to strengthen the fumes. I uncapped it, held the bottle to my nostril, sniffed deeply and held my breath as I went slightly cross-eyed, braced against the pounding in my chest, strong as a baby's kicks, my underwater heartbeat thumping in my ears. I lay back and closed my eyes. My temples and cunt throbbed and I felt a surge of sexual power. The blank, blotchy yellow screen of my eyelids gave way to a windowless office and a soldier, and as I pictured crouching before him, fishing out his soft bits and tearing into his scrotum with my teeth like into a tomato, I pleasured myself. I imagined feeling flooded in the hot blood and coiled noodles spilling from his groin, the ripped skin in my teeth, the smack of a bullet entering my forehead, blotting out my third eye, and I pleasured myself. Soldiers zipping my corpse in a body bag, ditching me in some overgrown valley, and I astonished myself, still hectically rubbing, not undeterred but fueled by the vile montage. Sometimes it got so bad, the images so hideous and demonic, a rushing cascade of intrusive thoughts I couldn't stop or control, I had to pinch my clit hard to shut it up.

Usually, though, I could bear it, like I did now, slumped into the couch cushion with a leg on the coffee table. I shook the bottle and took another hit. I resisted the ghastliest of the images and toyed with the most seductively extreme, going past the line, but not so far past that I scared myself in a lingering way. My breathing became frenetic as I raised my hips off the couch and held myself there, tensed euphorically. Afterward, I fell back and immediately began coughing, heaving, honking, stomach-clenching coughs of disgust. I swore I'd throw out the poppers and be done with them, but they were just expensive enough that I didn't want to be wasteful. And anyway, I'd tried that before.

The heat of the sunlight and the lack of AC felt suffocating. I wanted to crawl out of my skin. I texted Wadiyeh and told her to meet me at Beit Aneeseh, then I sent Lucía the same message. I washed my face and held it close to the mirror, staring at the peach fuzz above my lips. I licked my fingers and smoothed my eyebrows, picked a fluff of lint from my belly button, wrapped my hair in a cinnamon turban, and dropped the poppers in my purse in case we ended up dancing.

At Beit Aneeseh, thorny bushes with sparse pink roses lined one side of the perimeter wall near the table where Wadiyeh sat in a rattan chair waving to me. There were tables full of smug, laugh-happy Europeans. By now I'd made acquaintances with a few regulars at the bar, worldly Arabs born there but who'd traveled or studied outside and spoke smooth, arrogant English. There was occasionally an air of a superiority complex in the subdued but condescending way they talked to waitstaff or in happenstance bar conversation with working-class shebab. But most were so well adjusted and sweet it made me uncomfortable to be around them, so I sought refuge with the garish, vacuous, ridiculous Wadiyeh, who carried herself like a Ramallah socialite.

Sitting alone sipping argileh, an apple ornamenting the glowing wafer of coal, her perfume smelled like makeup, or her makeup was perfumed, I wasn't sure, but either way she was wearing too much of it. The smell mingled unpleasantly with the cloud of apple tobacco funneling out of her nostrils. I leaned over to kiss her cheeks and plopped down on the rattan chair beside her. There were days I liked how she smelled, powdery and synthetically floral, but tonight she smelled sweet and oily like a cadaver, like my father's puffy hands and face smelled when I leaned over the glossy wood casket to kiss him.

Some days she wore hijab, but mostly she didn't. Tonight she didn't. It depended on where we were going, if it matched a certain outfit or if it would make her fieldwork as an arts and culture journalist easier. I liked that about her, at least, her flippant stance on wearing hijab. More often than not she used a loose, stylized scarf over her hair as an excuse to wear tighter jeans and heels. I found this obnoxious and told her so. She clapped back that I dressed like I didn't care.

On one of our first nights out together she said I looked like a man, criticizing my lack of eyeshadow or lipstick and how my few pieces of jewelry were too reserved. Then I showed her the Snapchat filter that masculinized her face. She raised the phone eye level and posed as the image on her screen thickened her brow and added a digital beard along her jawline, and she cackled when she saw herself on the phone screen – a stabbing, throaty laugh. I said she looked like a himbo but she didn't hear or didn't get the joke, swiveling her head to try to outmaneuver the lush black facial hair that clung digitally to her face.

Lucía would be meeting us soon. A couple tables over, three shebab were chain-smoking and drinking amber bottles of Taybeh, their black hair gelled and crispy. One of them had a reddish-brown face and shyness in his yellowed eyes. He probably labored outside, I thought, unlike his olive-skinned friends who looked like salesmen or bank clerks in chunky silver watches, pointy leather shoes and boxy untucked dress shirts with starched collars. Another sheb at their table smiled at us, raised his beer bottle and nodded, and I told Wadiyeh we should suggest joining tables. She hesitated, but I could tell they were her type and she wanted to flirt.

'Come on,' I said, opening Snapchat, 'we can make them women.'

'I don't wanna embarrass them,' Wadiyeh laughed.

'They're not Wahhābī,' I said. 'They can take a joke.'

'I'm not even buzzed yet.'

She opened her phone camera to check her lipstick and swigged her beer, steeling herself. It was absurd – no matter how well the night went, how charming or persuasive the men, I knew Wadiyeh wouldn't go home with any of them. She was too prudish to even give them her number.

I nodded in their direction. 'Bidkum tokudu ma'ana?'

They lifted their beers and cigarette packs and dragged their table over so it touched ours. Wadiyeh pointed at each of their chests to get their names, reducing the grown men to giggling schoolboys waiting their turn. She talked too much like always, introducing me as 'sahebti Americaniyeh'. I would have rolled my eyes, but I didn't want to undermine her. Now that they were closer, I saw that the red-faced one, Majid, wore a wedding ring. He was handsome and had full lips and a part in his gelled hair.

Years of coming to Palestine had taught me that most villages had an unofficial troubadour, a young man everyone would nominate, if they could, to audition for *Arab Idol* to become the next Mohammed Assaf. Majid's friends did this now, cajoling him to impress us with his gift. The red deepened through the brown as he smiled nervously and declined. But when Wadiyeh rested her hand on his forearm and begged in a moany, childish tone, 'Bidna nismaa sotak al-hilo,' he cleared his throat and looked at the other tables as if to gauge how quiet or loud he should be. His friends stared at him with the anticipation of watching their favorite striker line up to take a penalty shot. He tilted his chin and sang a sad song, stretching the vowels with yearning vibrato. His voice was cottony and achingly gentle. He closed his eyes through some of it, then opened them and gazed absently at the sky. He held eye contact with me for a few seconds before looking around at the others. I wondered if he made his wife wet by singing to the TV with a cigarette dangling from his fleshy lower lip, if he whispered a song after coming another kid into her on a Wednesday, stuffed zucchini jostling around their bellies like the soggy clothes in the dryer.

After a round of fawning applause that included several of the surrounding tables, we settled back into conversation and a few minutes later, Wadiyeh opened Snapchat, flipped the camera and pointed it at me, showing the shebab my glitchy beard and thick caricaturesque eyebrows. They burst into guffaws, spurting smoke, the scent of apple and beer in the cool air. I thought I looked hot, honestly, if too metrosexual. We showed them what they'd look like as women, eyelashes like centipede legs. They ducked out of the frame, and Wadiyeh chased them with the front-facing camera, capturing their happy female faces, computerized hair draping over blushing cheekbones, lips full and red. I was irritated with her for monopolizing the male sheb-himbos' attention, and irritated with Majid for falling for it.

I ordered olives for the table. They came in a white saucer, swimming in brine, slippery and bruise-purple. I hogged the plate and ate most of them, dropping the pits into Wadiyeh's empty beer bottle. I picked up one of Majid's olive pits that he'd left sitting on the table next to his last beer and popped it in my mouth, turning it on my tongue like a Werther's.

Lucía arrived, Lucía the lesbian's lesbian in torn jeans and a slouchy yellow tank top, a single skinny dreadlock on one side of her caramel-colored hair. She made a show of kissing everyone three times, even the shebab she'd just met, from cheek to cheek to cheek. A soft-spoken waiter came over and she ordered a Riesling and a fresh argileh for the table. I was glad because now we would all pass the nozzle around and share each other's spit. Wadiyeh and the shebab flirtatiously debated what flavor of tobacco to order, but they settled on tufahtayn, the usual.

I slightly resented Lucía's ease with new people. She lounged back in her chair and spoke rapidly to one of the men and was nodding and laughing with him in under a minute. She even spoke Arabic more fluently than me, the bitch. I could picture her living her whole life in Palestine, where I was sure that even if I could, I probably wouldn't. I was here on a renewable three-month tourist visa, her work visa extended a year at a time. Still, I wished she'd break up with her girlfriend in Spain so I could start sleeping with her. Maybe I'd sleep with her anyway.

Lucía waved over a friend she recognized from across the bar, a drunk, pudgy Egyptian in a frumpy leather jacket. As he made his way to us, zigzagging widely around tables, she told us that they'd been in Tahrir Square together during the beginning of the so-called Arab Spring. She stood to greet him but he staggered past her and leaned over the table, jostling it and spilling the olive brine as he declared, in heavily accented English and without so much as a hello, 'We Egyptians are more Palestinian than you Palestinians. You can drink to forget but I can't.'

Wadiyeh sucked in air. No one spoke.

'Maalek, ya zalameh?' one of the sheb finally shouted, *What's wrong with you?*, as Majid grabbed his beer bottle menacingly. Lucía was panicking. I could see it in her eyes. She grabbed her drunk friend by his leather jacket and pulled him away as he smirked and muttered with wet lips.

Wadiyeh and I glanced at each other. She looked grim. I tried thinking of something to say to lighten the mood, anything to steer us away from the possibility of talking politics. I almost asked Majid for another song. Then the waiter came over and set Lucía's wine glass in front of her empty chair, and a minute later returned with the apple argileh, handing me the nozzle. He flipped the blazing coal with silver tongs and said, 'Fadhul.'

Wadiyeh was the only one who thanked him.

I hesitated, then held the plastic to my lips and inhaled, pulling in sweet vapor. The water in the base of the argileh burbled obscenely against the silence. ∎

BOMBED IN BEIRUT

Myriam Boulos

Introduction by Granta

'The voice of the bombs scares me a lot,' Mariama Fofanah told the Beirut-born photographer Myriam Boulos, who set up a small studio in a shelter where migrant workers from Sierra Leone found fleeting respite in the wake of the Israeli war on Lebanon. By September 2024 the assault had already produced a gruesome catalogue of images: the carefree detonation of entire villages, hands with missing fingers from pager attacks, moon-like craters where bunker bombs had reduced buildings and their inhabitants to dust, which filled the nostrils of the survivors. One of the most indelible images of the invasion was a variation on an already cemented genre, mock-the-victim photography, in the tradition of Abu Ghraib: a group of smiling Israeli soldiers pose, as if for a class reunion picture, with a large photograph of an elderly Lebanese woman which they have looted from an apartment. What to do as a photographer in a war where even simple family portraits have become trophies?

Boulos asked herself how to document the destruction in Lebanon, particularly the plight of those displaced by Israeli forces: 'Many photojournalists have been photographing people on the streets, sleeping or awake, stripped of any privacy or agency,' Boulos told *Granta*. 'A man in front of Ramlet El Bayda told me he would beat up anyone who tried to photograph him.' By November the death toll exceeded 3,000, with more than 185 children killed.

Boulos visited a shelter established by her sister and sister in law's friend, Déa Hage-Chahine, who had put up tents for domestic staff whose employers' homes were no longer habitable. The easy way to look at these women is as double victims: first, as the cogs of the kafala system in Lebanon which has cycled migrant labor through its society for seventy years, exchanging basic rights in return for employment at the whim of 'sponsors'; second, as targets for Israeli forces.

Boulos wanted to register this double violence in a different way. She set up her camera, draped colored fabric for a background, and invited the women to be photographed however they wished to be represented. The direct Speedlight flash would not only illuminate faces, but also accentuate the immediacy and tentative relief of people taking a pause on the run from destruction. The mayhem in Lebanon was momentarily suppressed as hands were put on hips, elbows casually rested on companions' shoulders, and children were lovingly fed. One woman seeking a haven, Aminata, helped Boulos record names and accounts of displacement. Conversations started haltingly, then flowed. To be in the position of granting a modicum of agency to people beaten into a corner provokes its own set of questions, but the point for Boulos was to register that this, too, was part of the war: on top of an old injustice there squatted a suffocating, engineered emergency. People who had made the long journey from Freetown to Beirut to make a little money were lucky to be returning home with their lives. ■

Thank you to Kadiatou Kamara, Mariama Fofanah, Mariatu Kabila, Adama Koroma, Kadiatu Tu Ray, Mariam Kamara, Fatmata Bai Koroma, Kumba Kamara, Maryisatu Koroma, Musu Kanu, Mariatu Swariay and her son Mohammad.

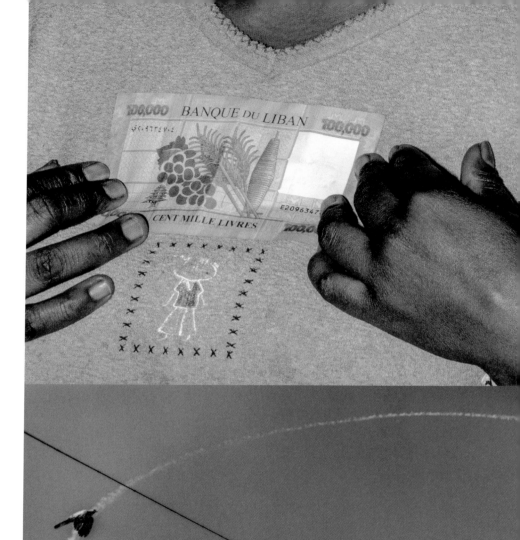

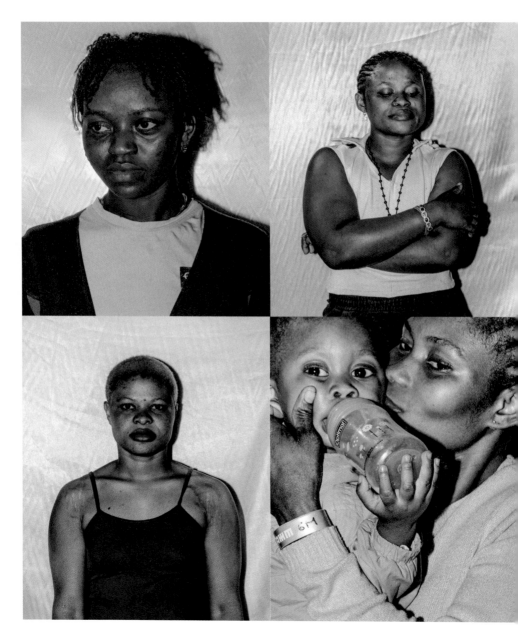

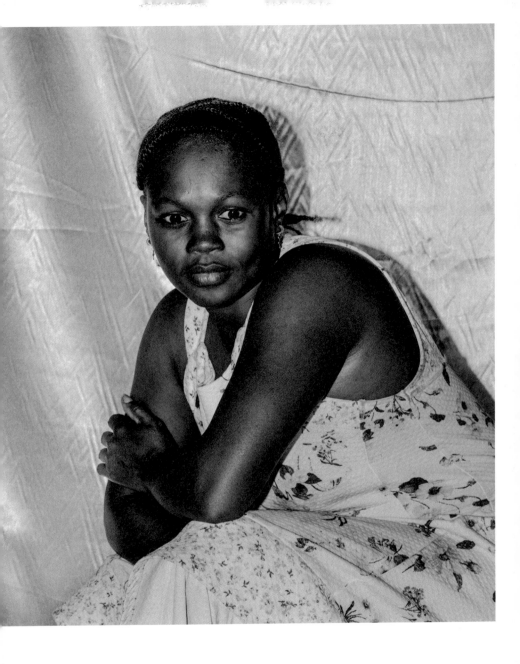

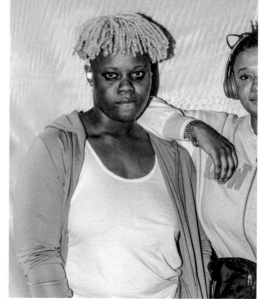

The voice of the bombs scares me a lot
I'm grateful that [...] with the African
girls and grateful [...] Mary, Lea and
Dia who provide [...] facilities.
I don't know about the KAFALA system!
I want the World [...] that I need help,
to have more [...] money,
to rent a house [...] beautiful people
I came to Lebanon [...] you in Africa.
in 2023.

Life in Lebanon is hard
because I am far from my family.

Yes, because I have friends Mary & Lea and
because of them, I feel at home.
Yes, it's my 1st time [...]
Because in the camp here [...] suffer and
I'm with the African girls
I don't know what happened to the house
No, I don't want to stay

Creative Writing and Literature

Study part-time with Oxford

Develop your own creativity or examine that of others with a short course or part-time qualification from one of the world's oldest and largest communities of part-time adult learners.

Short courses in Oxford and online
- Workshops and day schools
- Weekend events
- Weekly learning courses
- Summer schools in Oxford

Part-time qualifications
- Certificate of Higher Education
- Certificate in English Literature
- Diploma in Creative Writing
- MSt in Creative Writing
- MSt in Literature and Arts

SCAN TO LEARN MORE

@OxfordConted
www.conted.ox.ac.uk/granta2025

THE HURT BUSINESS

Declan Ryan

There's always a distinct charge before any fight, but it's different with heavyweights, especially these heavyweights. Anthony Joshua and Daniel Dubois are both big hitters, both woundable, beatable. The expectation is that, probably quite soon, one of the men currently giving each other unbroken eye contact in the ring will be unconscious. There's an appetite for it tonight, with the lights on and Wembley Stadium's arch above us, the songs sung, the fireworks and sparklers and LED wrist-lights dwindled to a solitary point of focus. We're three hours and five bouts in, and all of it has been leading up to Joshua vs Dubois. At this point of the night we just want harm done on our behalf.

Dubois made his entrance to the sound of drums, walking behind masked performers spinning flaming circles, in a Mike Tyson-inspired black poncho, black shorts, black boots. If he didn't quite manage to glower, he at least looked focused, as his entrance song, 'Lucifer Son of the Morning', a dubby reggae number, drew muted boos. Then came Joshua, all in white, as 'Oh Anthony Joshua' filled the stadium, chanted to the tune of 'Seven Nation Army'. Such is Joshua's star power, his seat-filling charisma, that Dubois – despite holding the title of 'world champion' – agreed to walk to the ring first tonight, usually the role of the challenger. As he walked, the sense of anticipation grew – if not bloodlust, then an outsourced potency, a collective will, for this strolling giant to get in there and do some damage for us. Now, Joshua gives his opponent an unblinking glare as he readies himself for – he hopes – restitution.

Anthony Joshua has been filling stadiums for nearly a decade. He rose to prominence as one of the poster boys of the London 2012 Olympic Games, winning Super Heavyweight gold at just twenty-two years old. From the beginning, he was an advertiser's dream – enormous, aggressively handsome, with a physique that suggested tectonic plates. He had enough backstory to make him seem gritty – a bit of drug dealing, trouble with the police, boxing as the straight path towards his new-found love of a motivational truism – but not so much to be off-putting or divisive. He'd only started boxing at eighteen, the age many boxers consider going pro. Within five years he'd beaten the best of his fellow amateurs and won that London gold – an extraordinarily rapid rise, testament to his ability to absorb and act on instruction, as well as his natural athleticism, determination and explosive punching power.

Joshua might have had a reputation as a star boy, but there were always doubters who pointed to his late start, suggesting it might prove his undoing as he ascended the ranks. He never had the amateur schooling most of his peers enjoyed – the junior years, in gloves too big for the growing frame; those long months in cold gyms, transmuting repetitive drills into muscle memory. His early style relied, instead, on ferocity: fast hands, brutalising combinations of punches which blasted his early opponents out, delivering the *coup de grâce*, usually, with his preternaturally concussive right hand. His rudimentary grasp of the essentials didn't matter when he could hit that hard, that often. The purists could complain that his movements were a little robotic, or that his footwork was wrong, after they woke up.

Over the years, however, Joshua's star power has threatened to outstrip his skill in the ring; fans connected immediately with the man's story, his persona, his humbly arresting feats. He has never been a skulking, threatening sort of fighter; he doesn't go in for trash talk or baby-threatening, so much as old-fashioned respect, fair play, parliamentary procedure. In his early twenties, he was still living with his mother, in Watford, and you got the sense that while he would knock people out, he'd feel bad afterwards. After his gold medal, lots were cast for everything that went on or into his hulking frame, with clothing brands, headphones, sports drinks and other conglomerates ensuring his leaving the house required rigorous planning. He turned professional with an expectation that he'd stroll through his first dozen fights. And that's largely what happened – but not just because of Joshua. It happened because of the team around him, which matchmade and built Joshua into an unmissable attraction, handpicking opponents to highlight his best aspects, and keep any flaws well hidden.

Matchmaking is one of the most important tasks for the team behind a fighter – it's a dark art, picking the right tests. There's no fixture list in boxing, and few demands are ever made at an organisational level that can't be negotiated around. Joshua's potential – as a fighter, but also as a brand, a commodity, was apparent already in his Olympic days. The last thing the brains behind his operation wanted was to risk pushing him into deep waters too soon, before he'd learned more of the tricks of the trade, or developed an ability to navigate the longer duration of professional fights, to compete in contests where the aim wasn't to score points but to end the night as early as possible. 'You don't get paid overtime in boxing' is a familiar, pragmatic, adage.

His promoter, Eddie Hearn, and the wider team behind him, had one chief goal: to make him, and themselves, as much money as possible while taking as few risks as they could get away with, at least until he had made it to the top of the mountain. His education was important, but far more important was gilding his box-office appeal, preserving his unbeaten record, and maximising his ability to wow fans in highlight reels of him putting tall men on their backs, out for the count.

Those hoped-for knockouts came, but with them went the chances of Joshua amassing big-fight experience, or gauging the limits of his stamina. Instead, Joshua's early professional career followed the age-old pattern of any bankable prospect, especially in the heavyweight division, where one clean shot can ruin everything. In the tried and tested manner of any hot up-and-comer, he was fed baggy men in kit from the lost and found, served up to fall down. And if he mostly struggled to get out of first or second gear, the men who might be able to challenge him to do so, to raise his game, were kept away, too risky a proposition while he was finding his feet as a pro.

Boxing is still the Wild West of sport. FIFA, in football, may have its grave flaws, but at least it gives the appearance of some centralised order, of an adult – however nefarious – being somewhere in the room. In boxing, there is no overarching global authority. Instead, four main sanctioning bodies each award their own belts, creating a multitude of 'world champions'. This means that at any one time there can be (at least) four fighters with a claim to being the 'world champion' in their weight class. A canny promoter, such as Hearn, thrives on this ambiguity, and will capitalise on this proliferation of worlds by targeting the weaker 'champions' to fight against his hot prospects.

The system is so opaque that the fighters' rankings can effectively be bought, or at least bargained over, at annual conventions by their promoters. A promoter might say, 'My fighter deserves a title shot. You may disagree, but perhaps this money will change your mind.' Business interests often take precedence over sporting ones, to the point where the leading fighters of their day need never fight one another to prove their superiority, but can instead enjoy lucrative and garlanded careers, claiming throughout to be the best in the world, while facing only hand-picked opponents unlikely to expose their weaknesses. Think of what tennis would be if Federer could have chosen never to play Nadal, and you're getting there. Now picture it happening in casinos, late at night, with funding from people with links to organised crime, and big bets riding on the outcome. Shockingly, there have been instances of corruption over the years.

The worst thing to happen to Joshua early in his career was his victory against the hapless American Charles Martin, a woefully reluctant opponent wearing what appeared to be his daughter's shorts, who just so happened to be in possession of a world title. By defeating him, Joshua became a 'champ', but the title came too early. His education, until that point a process of learning on the job, was abruptly curtailed. With the belt around his waist, Joshua was a ticket-shifting cash cow, with several capable suitors wanting to test his lucrative mettle.

In boxing, there's a constant balancing act going on. If, as a promoter, you're in charge of someone with Joshua's earning power, who can routinely sell out stadiums, the last thing you want to do is allow that gravy train to hit the buffers before it's made you a fortune. Fighters who make the forgivable mistake of merely being good at the sport, but not achieving some sort of wider, marketable profile, are often filed in the 'who needs him' club. For promoters these are the boxers who pose a real risk of beating their star, while not offering anything like the sort of money it would require to take that chance. These sorts of dangerous propositions can – thanks to the freedom promoters get to matchmake and cherry-pick – be avoided, perhaps indefinitely, or at least until they manoeuvre their way to being a mandatory challenger in the eyes of one of the sanctioning bodies. Becoming a 'mandatory' means the boxer in possession of the belt has to agree to fight you, or hand back his title. But deals can be struck, 'step-aside' money paid. Even then, promoters can often find a way around giving challengers a shot at their prize possession – 'they don't bring enough to the table', 'we're going a different way', etc. Honour, or anything approaching it, sits vanishingly low on the priority list.

But at some point you have to take the brakes off, or at least appear to. Otherwise, the public mood is liable to sour as fans begin to suspect that your star has been too mollycoddled. The trick is to pair him with people who are *almost* as good as him – fighters with enough name recognition for the occasion – while avoiding the ones who are as good or better for as long as possible, especially during those prime earning years.

As a fighter moves up the ranks, activity also decreases. In their early days, they might fight five or six times per year, largely against soft targets. But by the time they become a prominent name, a headliner, the frequency can dwindle to two or even one fight per year, such is the massive marketing and promotional effort required to hype each of their events. For Joshua, this meant that it wasn't until 2017, at the age of twenty-seven, five years into his professional career and in his nineteenth fight, that he faced his first significant test in a fight at Wembley against the Ukrainian Wladimir Klitschko.

Since Floyd Mayweather's time at the top of the sport, remaining unbeaten has become a sought-after, and heavily protected, status in boxing – often at the expense of meaningful pairings between leading fighters. Mayweather was a remarkable fighter, but even his final years became testament to preserving his record rather than taking risks. On the whole, going unbeaten for a decade or longer is more likely to mean you've avoided your chief rivals than that you're a generational talent. This is one of the reasons why Anthony Joshua and Tyson Fury – the two standout British heavyweights of their generation – have never fought one another, despite all their overlapping years at the summit. That fight would break all financial records, especially if it happened in the UK. It has *almost* happened several times but, in the 'red-light district of sport', nothing is guaranteed until the bell goes and the fighters meet in the centre of the ring. Until then, injuries happen, contracts collapse, promotions fall apart.

This version of purity was never set at such a premium in the past – the great fighters showed their mettle through how they recovered from their defeats. Sugar Ray Robinson, arguably the greatest boxer of all time, avenged a loss to Jake LaMotta twenty-one days later in February 1943. Even more staggeringly to post-war eyes, he managed to fit in a tune-up fight between the two bouts. Today, the rarity of fights and the fear of losing them go hand in hand.

The 2017 fight against Klitschko was the first real risk to Joshua's unbeaten record. Klitschko, another former Olympic gold medallist, was the real thing. If nagging worries about Joshua's durability or skill were valid, this fight was sure to expose them. What occurred was an instant classic – Joshua won, after an up-and-down battle, halting a flagging Klitschko in the eleventh. However, the win came with revelations. Joshua had shown he could be hurt – badly – and that his gas tank took an age to refill, time he might not be granted by sprightlier opposition. People started to wonder out loud if all those muscles were a hindrance. Klitschko was forty-one. What would happen if Joshua had been in similarly dire straits against a younger, hungrier man?

Joshua's first and most traumatic loss came in the spring of 2019, at the hands of a man whose hunger bordered on carnal. On what was meant to be his triumphant American debut at Madison Square Garden, Joshua met the near-spherical Mexican American fighter Andy Ruiz Jr, who was greeted with pity, scorn or incredulity as he entered the ring. Ruiz, at least to people who'd never seen him fight, seemed an unserious proposition. Dismissed as a lazy, demotivated or generally unthreatening fighter, Ruiz nevertheless defeated and concussed Joshua in one of the biggest upsets in the history of the sport, his fast hands and unexpectedly nimble footwork giving Joshua conniptions.

Joshua's career can be divided into two distinct eras: before and after his loss to Ruiz. While he avenged that shocking defeat later that same year, and reclaimed his title belts in the process, he emerged from the ordeal a different, more cautious, at times even reluctant fighter. It was now understood that Joshua had the potential to unravel – to his winning smile and explosive right hand was added an even more appealing quality: an air of fragility. In a sport that strongly favours the home fighter, the marquee name, the possibility that Joshua might unravel against someone who wasn't an obvious destroyer, that he might find a way to lose even with all his advantages – athletic and otherwise – now gave his fights a compulsive tension. And there would always be something in the British sports fan's psyche that favoured the flawed over the impervious, that gravitated towards the one who – perched on the brink of glory – could supply the ingredients for his own poignant undoing.

Joshua cycled through several trainers in an effort to backfill his technical nous. Trainers are key to every fighter, but for Joshua – the late-adopter, the non-natural – they're more important than most. In action, he tends to hang on the cornermen's every word between rounds, fighting precisely to instruction, incapable of the in-fight flowing improvisation which marks out those boxers whose movements were hard-wired at a much younger age. For a while, Joshua's newfound self-protective streak came at the cost of what had made him such an eye-catching knockout merchant. The memory of Ruiz still fresh, he was less willing to take necessary risks to subdue opponents.

Joshua seemed stuck. He hoped to evolve into a more mature, defensively sound heavyweight but had lost the fire – and firepower – of old. He was out-thought and defeated by the balletic Oleksandr Usyk, twice, despite being the much bigger man. On those nights, there was a sense that had he been a bit more willing to take risks, to go for broke, he might have troubled the Ukrainian stylist. Instead, he lost a battle of skill, without really making a dent. Second-guessing himself, Joshua seemed to have lost his edge.

Around October 2023, Joshua started working with Ben Davison, a chirpy Essex-based smiler. Davison, his fifth trainer in two years, seemed to have found the right formula, reconnecting Joshua with his inner finisher. In March 2024, he fought the former UFC star Francis Ngannou. As a confidence-building exercise, it couldn't have gone better. Ngannou, for all his combat experience, was a novice in the boxing ring, and Joshua treated him as such. He dominated, walking through Ngannou and almost beheading him. Had Joshua finally cracked it? Had he reconnected with that KO specialist of old but with added seasoning, a bit more hard-earned wisdom?

No one can really tell how good a fighter is until it's all over – while they go on, there's always that chance of the redemptive comeback, the unlikely, against-all-odds victory snatched from defeat. Joshua is entering the legacy phase now, the defining period. He hasn't proved to be the untouchable steamroller he seemed to be in those early years, but nor is he the fragile, overprotected charlatan he risked morphing into after his blow-up against Ruiz. Most likely, at thirty-five, he doesn't have another big rebuild left in him.

And so we find ourselves here tonight. Daniel Dubois might not be *the* world champion, but he is *a* champion, and if Joshua can beat him, and look good while doing it, he will have enough momentum to merit a tilt at one or both of the other giants of his era, Tyson Fury and Oleksandr Usyk. The time was right for him to march on, now, to have a final say in cementing the way we'd look back at him.

It will all build from what happens tonight then, at Wembley; this last, defining, era of Joshua. This mega-event was only possible because of an influx of capital from Saudi Arabia. As part of an attempted rebrand, the Saudis have, over the last few years, bid to become major players in boxing, co-opting the sport as part of a seemingly endless 'Riyadh Season' – a raft of entertainments designed to paint the nation as a come-one, come-all tourist destination. For decades, a number of the best possible fights in boxing have proved impossible to make happen due to promotional and TV network rivalries, and other frustrating, fan-denying politics. The Saudis, led by Turki Alalshikh, chairman of their General Entertainment Authority, have thawed these cold wars, to a point where insoluble bigwigs such as promoters Frank Warren and Eddie Hearn can be photographed holding hands, looking like lottery winners who've waived their right to anonymity. Riyadh Season is now branching out and aiming high, wanting a bit of the famous English atmosphere. One of the downsides of the events in Saudi Arabia has been the subdued energy in arenas filled with invited celebrities and local dignitaries but lacking the boozed-up rabble-rousers needed to create

the familiar late-night racket. Tonight, Wembley has been transformed
into a temporary outpost of Saudi soft power. Adverts encouraging
us all to visit Riyadh play on an endless loop between fights, and
lovingly produced brochures have been arranged at the bar.

There are few fighters now who aren't hoping to catch the eye
of Alalshikh, drawn by the promise of their own turn under lights
at this wattage, and cheques they couldn't otherwise dream of. Yet,
it wasn't until Liam Gallagher took to the stage before the headline
fight, rasping through three Oasis songs, that Wembley felt packed
out. If the reported 96,000 seats – a figure which would make it the
biggest-selling boxing event in post-war Europe – had all been sold,
as we had been told all week, a lot of their buyers must have been
detained, or forgetful. The air of 1990s nostalgia Gallagher brought
was apt given the talk all week comparing the fight to Lennox Lewis's
1993 bout with Frank Bruno, one of the last – and most notable –
times two Brits contested a world heavyweight title. That night a
beefed-up Bruno came unstuck, after a bright start, unravelling at
the hands of the younger, more skilled Lewis. Now we are witnessing
a new generation of UK big men, as they act out those familiar roles
of challenger and champion.

Daniel Dubois, Joshua's opponent this time, is a fellow Brit,
but their similarities end there. Dubois first caught the attention of
boxing fans as a teenager, amid rumours he'd knocked out Joshua in
sparring, when he was just nineteen and Joshua twenty-six. As with all
sparring scuttlebutt, details were hazy and conflicting, the *Omertà* of
the gym difficult to penetrate. Apparently, this kid was a real puncher,
a danger-man, the next one. Unlike Joshua, he didn't go down the
amateur Olympic route. He turned professional early, opting to
punch for pay, rather than sink years into linking up with Team GB,
earning a pittance and hoping to earn a place in the Olympic squad.
Former Olympians tend to transition to far greater fanfare, and far
larger signing-on fees, than those who choose to fast track towards the
professional side of the sport. The Olympic fights allow them to get to
compete against most of their future opponents, over three rounds,

in far-flung locations and with very few eyes on them. And Olympic champions achieve a clarity almost never found in the professional ranks – proving themselves the sole best at their weight, in their time. But even Olympic champions must start fresh as pros – adjusting to a longer, more gruelling format and facing unpredictable opponents. These fighters, who were never given government funding to hone their skills, are often less refined but they can be more dangerous – resentful, wily, survivors, keen to leave a mark on their hot-housed and fast-tracked counterparts.

On the face of it, Dubois has been offered up to Joshua to get him back to the top table. He is seen by those in the Joshua business as another in the line of those tantalisingly beatable champs. He offers Joshua a quick route towards being able to call himself (and earn the wages of) a champion again. Admittedly, his belt was won not in the ring but via email, boxing being one of the few sports whose governance resembles a phishing scam. Oleksandr Usyk, having beaten Tyson Fury to briefly hold all four heavyweight belts, was almost immediately stripped of one because he chose to honour a planned rematch against Fury rather than agreeing to fight Dubois, his mandatory challenger. With the belt vacant, Dubois became a 'world champion' by default, having been sitting in the chair when the music stopped. Dubois's title got him the payday dream ticket of fighting Joshua at Wembley, but he didn't really belong in his company, did he? Wasn't there something a little bit second-rate about him? Had you seen him being *interviewed*?

Both are in the ring, now. Dubois pacing back and forth, always staring directly at Joshua, who seems less willing to go in for any of this fronting out. Dubois is keeping himself warm, bouncing on his toes, having had to wait for his opponent. Joshua looks zoned in, used to it all, staring somewhere into the distance. Dubois's mouth opens, flashing his black gumshield. The referee is between them, giving final instructions, before standing back to let them go. As the fight begins, it's clear this is a confident, unloosed Joshua – that he, like most of the crowd, believes he operates on a different plane to his opponent.

Joshua holds his left hand low, his chin high and unguarded, and acts like Dubois is a problem he'll soon, simply, solve. Dubois comes out looking to punch respect into him, taking the centre of the ring, leading with stiff left jabs – his key weapon – range-finding but spiteful, keeping Joshua at bay and stinging him as he does so. Within thirty seconds Dubois lands the first meaningful punch, a strong right hand which Joshua felt, dipping against the ropes, clenched up, affronted. The round continues in the same vein – Dubois poking, Joshua casual, on low-alert.

Dubois, despite choosing to cash in aged nineteen, was far from green, thanks to years of tutelage from his boxing-obsessed father Dave Dubois, a former market trader. Dubois was training at the Peacock Gym in Canning Town from the age of nine, but had started being put through his paces from a much younger age at home. His childhood was spartan. Home-schooled, strait-laced, thinly socialised, the Dubois who emerged on the main stage was a long way from the branded, beaming spokesman Joshua. He seemed more like an oversized, awkward boy, being pushed too fast on his bike towards a motorway. Yet there was no doubting his talent. He had fast hands, a sharp, well-tuned jab, and he clearly hit hard – as his early victims quickly discovered.

However, as Dubois did start to step up and be met with media scrutiny, something felt a bit off. His father's overbearing influence was unsettling: those infant workouts, the other siblings also conscripted into the hurt business, the chatter that he didn't really get out much, own a phone, or – really – seem to want to be doing this at all. In interviews, journalists struggled to get much out of him, beyond a minor remix of 'I'm ready to fight. Let's go.' There's something to be said for letting one's fists do the talking, but tell that to the T-shirt vendors, or the sponsors.

Doubts about Dubois's potential were seemingly confirmed in 2020 when he quit in the tenth round against Joe Joyce, taking a knee for the referee's full count of ten, effectively conceding. The fact that the orbital bone in Dubois's eye socket had been fractured seemed, in discussion afterwards, an afterthought. Boxers, with their 'warrior code', are expected to 'go out on their shield'. The sort of maiming which would see the average citizen scream for an air ambulance is – in the course of a boxing match – supposed to be dealt with via a combination of stoicism and whatever can be resolved through the application of a rough towel. Dubois, in choosing to protect his sight and long-term health, had proven his critics right. The comeback heaped on further degradation. He won a spurious, minor belt and soon after got a shot at the seriously-big-time, against Oleksandr Usyk, but again ended the night on a knee, quitting for a second time, and further reinforcing the hunch that when the going got tough, he didn't. Immediately before this fight Dubois had hit a bit of good form and – possibly – managed to clamber over the mental block which saw him tap out on his two biggest nights. There was talk of him having come into himself, finally.

Now Dubois has a chance to step out from Joshua's shadow – where he has long lingered in terms of promotional weight, kudos and popular appeal. Could he strike a blow against the golden boy and claim some of Joshua's star power for himself? Or will Joshua show that his years of experience in the limelight are of greater advantage on this big occasion than Dubois's focused but unglamorous years of grinding away from the glare?

In the ring, with about twenty seconds left of the first round, Joshua's laissez-faire approach starts to create problems. He swings wildly, misses, and turns himself around with his momentum. Dubois responds by hurling a big right hand – like a fast bowler – which detonates on Joshua's chin, causing him to slump forwards, his gloves touching the canvas, momentarily a supplicant. Had there been more time in the round, that might have been it, but the bell rings. Joshua finds his stool, looking unsteady and dazed. Abashed, buzzed, he looks trapped in the middle of a nightmare. A minute to recover may not be long enough. Dubois comes out strong in the second round, landing clean shots that rock and wobble Joshua, who looks stiff and unstable. Yet, Dubois doesn't go hell for leather, wary perhaps of overcommitting. Meanwhile, Joshua's survival skills buy him a bit more time to recover his compromised senses.

The third round follows similar lines, a back-pedalling Joshua circles the ring, trying, sometimes unsuccessfully, to avoid Dubois's right hand. Dubois lands a couple of heavy shots, again rocking Joshua, but picks them cautiously, respectful of the fight-changing power still in Joshua's arsenal. As ever, Dubois looks functional rather than arresting. Even when he's dispatching someone, even when all the elements are there for something dazzling, the punches thud but there's no stardust on the gloves. Then, with about twenty seconds to go before the bell, Dubois lands a left on Joshua's temple that seems to short-circuit him. Joshua stumbles towards the ropes, legs tremblingly unreliable, and another punch forces him to touch down. A count is taken up – correctly – on the loudspeaker but not enforced by the referee, handing Dubois a chance to land more, unguarded, shots, bludgeoning Joshua to the floor, potshotting him on the ropes. For a moment it looks like this is it. But, somehow, Joshua manages to get up, presenting himself to the referee for approval. Only the fact that he is moments from another minute's rest allows him to be waved on. In the corner, his second presses ice to the back of his neck as he sits staring into space.

It now becomes a matter of seeing how Joshua's night will, finally, be resolved. Somewhere between the first and second rounds, he transformed from predator to prey, and now we are merely witnessing his capture, waiting for him to go to ground for good. As he comes out for the fourth round he is almost instantly down again. The referee appears to call off the fight, waving his hands in a gesture that ordinarily means 'it's done'. Instead, confusingly, he declares Joshua's trip to the canvas accidental. Joshua stands, crestfallen but defiant, tapping his big chest with his gloves to say, 'On we go.'

By now, the atmosphere has become discomfiting – voyeuristic, but in a way that feels darker, more charged. There is a feeling that, really, we shouldn't be watching this, that this level of humiliation is bad for us to witness. Joshua isn't just losing, he's being punished

– for his celebrity, his late start, his rediscovered confidence, his hapless bravery. And the one delivering the punishment? This quiet, dismissable non-star, this mumbling, charmless home-schooler, who knocked him down years back, and who has been itching ever since to get at him for real.

But the tide can turn quickly in a fight, on a single punch, any small sign of reinvigoration. Towards the end of the fourth round, Joshua lands his first significant shot of the night, a right on the jaw, giving Dubois pause and – fleetingly, dangerously – reintroducing hope. He couldn't, could he? This being heavyweight boxing, where one right hand can change it all, we are forced to imagine miracles. Maybe, somehow, he's been punched back to lucidity. Maybe Dubois has punched himself out?

If Joshua can land another right in the fifth, well, he's always been a clinical finisher. It's moments such as this – this sudden gear-shift, the spiralling possibilities, the imagined splintering of potential conclusions, which lends boxing its capacity for absolute immersion. From the feeling that we've accidentally put on a snuff film, to suddenly being back in the wish-fulfilment business.

And Joshua does seem brighter, more able to shrug off Dubois's punches. He lands a seismic right on Dubois's chin, forcing the younger man to step back, shakily. Joshua bounds on, sensing unlikeliest glory might be one punch off. As he moves into the corner where Dubois lurks he rolls the dice, throwing a right hand – a punch that, if it connects, will mean all is forgiven. Dubois throws his own right at the same time, and it has a shorter distance to travel. It hits Joshua's chin like a hammer and turns his lights out in an instant – he falls face forwards, straight down; a sleeping, slain, giant.

From where I'm sitting, high up enough to need the big screens, not so far I can't see the figures in the ring, it looked like an execution. Anthony Joshua down again, but this time not getting up. At least not in time to beat the referee's count. His last desperate gamble to turn the fight ended in a short right hand, a brutal punctuation mark. How have we got *here?* the stunned silence seems to say.

There's a lot of head-shaking going on around me, a lot of people angrily storming out. A large proportion of the crowd is up from their seats and down the aisles with Joshua barely back to his feet. Boos and thwarted expectations cascade around the cold stadium. Plastic pint glasses fly through the air, their spray going in all directions. Joshua has not just lost, he's been run over, knocked down four times, the last for the count, all in the space of less than five rounds. This isn't what people have paid to see.

In every sense, Joshua had seemed superior to Dubois coming in – his credentials, his gold, his charm, his crossover appeal. None of that came into the ring with him. There, he was forced to walk the only terrain where Dubois was more comfortable, and where, in the end, he knew more. It was Dubois who was sharper, quicker to the punch, lethal once encouraged. The first knockdown scrambled Joshua, and fighters when seriously hurt are forced to revert to untutored instinct, to base fundamentals. Joshua's let him down. He became a novice again, swinging for the fences, chin in the air, reliant on the raw materials which had once turned his life around, long before he was king. Dubois couldn't match him outside the ring – in accolades, popularity or polish – but inside, that didn't matter.

Before the fighters could leave there'd be a press conference – Joshua would be pushed on whether this was it, or if he'd carry on and try to avenge yet another loss, try to build back after this latest, and most diminishing, setback to date. A second fight with Dubois would make even more money now, for them both, after what had just happened. There would always be an appetite for him to fight Fury, however far both fighters drifted past their primes. But could Joshua, in good conscience, face the toil and sacrifice it would require to scale the heights again, after enduring all this, at the hands of someone he'd thought he'd handle comfortably? Perhaps it was time to cash in, to set out for the no-less-terrifying waters of a life without fighting.

He might also have to question the wisdom, once again, of those around him: the trainers who'd sent him out there with too cavalier a tactical plan, the promoters who chose this brooding, younger, ambitious foe for him, and had become even richer off the back of it. Boxing forces its participants to suspend their disbelief, to discount any evidence set against their omnipotence. He would have to answer these questions, and soon, his ears ringing, his bruises still coming out.

Not quite elite, then, if this was the final sum of it. But the tragedy of Joshua is that he's been, has always been, about 90 per cent of the way to greatness. If he could only sort out those remaining flaws, be a bit cannier, combine the early explosivity with this wiser head, he could yet, somehow, fight on until he gets what he's aimed for from the start – recognition as the best of his time. There might be another rematch, another rebuild, but for now there is only quiet, humility, a new world order. 'Are you not entertained?' Dubois barks on the microphone, flying high, trying out a bit of hype, to an almost empty stadium. But it's something heavier than entertainment. Dubois is that most dangerous thing, a man long drilled with a singular purpose, who has managed to organise things to happen on his terms. He doesn't need any of us. He's just taken apart the thing we loved the most – for this hour or two at least – and made us watch him do it, to show he could. ∎

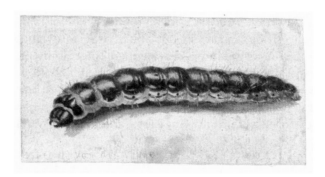

VINCENT LAURENSZ VAN DER VINNE
A Caterpillar, late seventeenth century

THE FIRST PERSON

Kathryn Scanlan

W here the path cuts left, a black caterpillar was on the ground –
on the move. It looked wooly and prickly and propelled itself
with speed.

I picked up a dry leaf, and when the caterpillar climbed aboard, I
carried the leaf to the safety of the grass and set it down at the base
of a tree.

A man had stopped to watch me. When I straightened with a satisfied
expression, the man was there, ready to pop my balloon. He pointed
and said, *They're everywhere* – but what he meant was, *What's the use?*

And I saw that, ahead, caterpillars charged the path in mass, away
from the trees, toward the busy road, all hellbent, it seemed, on the
same obscure destination.

Who was I to tell them otherwise?

I thought of the traffic-directing hummingbird who likes to bully
cars at the corner of Kirby and Bellwether. *Stop!* I could say to the
runners, bikers, dog-walkers and stroller-pushers who rolled up.

Watch your step!

But the man – this bald killjoy – was still watching me, and seemed to interpret my hesitation as interest in his sex.

Go on, I said to myself. I put one foot in front of the other.

I passed a person walking a small pig on a jeweled leash. When a jogger flew by, a drop of his sweat landed on my lip. Along an iron rail, a woman scraped shit from her shoe with a stick. In the path-people's faces and postures were expressions of ownership and isolation – *All of this is mine! – Get out of my way!* – and as usual, I was thinking about what I wanted, too: silk trousers, calfskin mules, gold chains – geraniums in Gainey pots – nice cheese and a bottle of Lambrusco – a comfortable couch – a comfortable house – a comfortable life.

At the end of the path – or anyway, at the place where I typically turn around – a child-sized car, wheels askew, was abandoned. LVNLRG, said the car's vanity plates.

Across the street, a man blasted spent white blossoms into massive dirt-plumes with the gas-powered blower strapped to his back.

The municipal trash bin smelled like a corpse.

The lake looked like a pewter platter.

When I returned to where the path cuts right, the crushed caterpillars were dirt-dulled and disfigured by the orange gut-bubbles that oozed from them. I stopped to look and was roughly shoulder-checked, without apology or acknowledgment, by a half-naked youth.

Then I spotted a lone figure, traveling. She was headed toward a patch of pigweed, which thrives in disturbed areas.

When fully extended, the caterpillar's shape is that of the bold *I* – the first person – the mark of one who devours in order to transform herself. ∎

NICOLAAS STRUYK
A Caterpillar and Two Moths on a Branch and Two Butterflies, early–mid eigteenth century

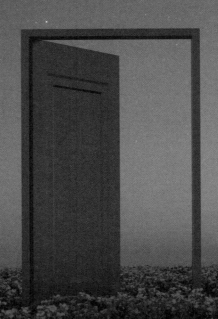

AESTHETICA
CREATIVE WRITING AWARD 2025

WIN £5000 & PUBLICATION
SUBMIT YOUR POETRY | FICTION

DEADLINE 31 AUGUST 2025

CHAMPION

Prarthna Singh

Introduction by Snigdha Poonam

In early 2001, Mahavir Phogat, an amateur wrestler and father of four daughters, ordered his eldest two, Geeta (eleven) and Babita (nine), to join him in a mud pit he had carved out in his courtyard in Balali, a small village in Haryana. The Olympic Committee had just announced women's wrestling as a competitive category, with the first matches slated for 2004, and Phogat wanted in on the game. For the next seven to eight years, Geeta and Babita trained daily to the point of exhaustion: long runs each morning, technique sessions throughout the day, and strength-building in the evenings using homemade equipment crafted by their father. One day they'd climb ropes, the next lift sandbags, and the day after drag tractor tyres.

To most people in the village, Phogat was just another madman – until the medals started coming in. Geeta went on to qualify for the 2012 Olympics in London, the first Indian woman to earn that honour. Babita clinched the gold medal in the 2014 Commonwealth Games in Glasgow. By then, the younger sisters had also been drafted.

Today, India is a major player in global wrestling, mainly thanks to the medals won by women athletes, whose presence on the mat was, until recently, widely regarded by traditionalists as unwelcome, even impure.

The wrestling arena was – and is – a celebration of brute strength and thigh-slapping, milk-glugging camaraderie, with its presiding deity, Hanuman, the monkey-warrior from the *Ramayana*, a lifelong bachelor who is ever-ready for a bout. Organisers of traditional wrestling events, called 'dangals', where men, clad in loincloths, battle in mud pits, in Haryana and elsewhere in northern India, historically did not allow women as spectators.

Change was somewhat driven by necessity. In families without sons to train, girls were pushed into the wrestling pits – and they thrived. Since Balali's rise to prominence, versions of the Phogat family's story have played out in many villages and towns in and around Haryana: a father or uncle picks a young girl in the family – sometimes all of them – to be trained as a wrestler. Their long hair is chopped off, wardrobes shift from loose salwar kameez to snug bodysuits, and domestic duties are partly replaced by squats and lunges. As often happens, physical fitness is more easily gained than social approval. Relatives warn parents that they're making their daughters 'unmarriageable'. Village committees call for boycotts. Mobs attack dangals that feature female wrestlers.

In response to the growing need for separate and safe training environments, akhadas exclusively for girls have emerged. These academies mostly draw their students from the rural backwaters in north-west India, where the harsh constraints of gender hold sway. In Haryana, which produces most of India's wrestlers, decades of female infanticide and selective abortions have severely skewed the sex ratio. Life for most girls here often follows a set pattern – an arranged marriage after high school, followed by a lifetime of domestic labour under strict male control. In her recently published memoir *Witness*, Sakshi Malik recalls her grandmother sharing how her mother-in-law would dilute the milk she was given to drink – 'for no other reason but to lower her self-worth'.

By 2022, Prarthna Singh had spent eight years photographing girls and women in wrestling. She met them at government-run training camps, where competitive wrestlers spend months preparing for selected events. It's not the preparation that stands out in her pictures – rather the quiet minutiae of life between training sessions. We see names scrawled on lockers, clothes hanging to dry on lines, chargers tucked into sockets.

Even when catching them in 'action' – flexing their muscles or performing a technique – the pictures juxtapose strength and vulnerability, as if the wrestlers are expressing the fragility of the chance they have to craft a life different from the one they left behind.

At the end of that year, she invited me to join her on a visit to a girls-only academy in Sonipat, Haryana. At the time, forty-five girls were training at Yudhveer Akhada across various levels. Most of them were dropped off here by their fathers. The youngest was ten years old.

When I asked what drew them to wrestling, many pointed to India's first Olympic medal in women's wrestling. In 2016's Rio Olympics, twenty-three-year-old Sakshi Malik shared a room with Vinesh Phogat, the niece of Mahavir Phogat and a three-time Commonwealth gold medallist. For both, it was their first Olympics, in separate weight classes. They had been close friends for several years. On the eve of the quarter-finals, after making the weight cut, they celebrated together with ready-to-eat Indian food: one held the pouch of curried rajma under hot water in the sink, while the other fetched bread from the Olympic kitchen.

Vinesh suffered one of the worst injuries of her career. But Sakshi won a nail-biting match against the redoubtable Aisuluu Tynybekova of Kyrgyzstan, bringing home the bronze. She received a welcome worthy of a national hero, with rewards and accolades from various governments and celebrations across the country. In her home state of Haryana, people danced in the streets.

An Olympic medal is more than a sporting prize. In an argument, it can serve as the final word. Sakshi's bronze was the answer parents now gave nosy relatives and village elders questioning their daughters' ambition. 'Today, go to any district in Haryana, and you will find a wrestling academy for girls every four to five kilometres. It gives me joy to acknowledge that my victory opened doors, changed mindsets,' Sakshi told me.

Shortly after Rio, a Bollywood blockbuster transformed even non-sports fans into admirers of women's wrestling. In December 2016, *Dangal* hit cinemas, with Aamir Khan starring as Mahavir Phogat. The Phogat family went on to produce one wrestling champion after another – not only Geeta and Babita but also Ritu, Sangeeta, Vinesh and Priyanka, the last two being daughters of Mahavir's late younger brother. A testament to Bollywood's influence, *Dangal* inspired countless families to seek out the nearest akhada willing to admit girls.

Siksha Kharb's father enrolled her at the Yudhveer academy in 2018, when she was eleven. 'After Sakshi *didi* won the medal, every second girl in my village wanted to become a wrestler,' she told me. Rounak Kumari left home when she was fifteen. 'Papa used to watch a lot of wrestling on the television. Because he didn't have a son, he used to make us, his five daughters, bout with each other at home. I was the oldest and the best at the game.' *Dangal* was a household favourite. 'Initially, he dropped me at a different wrestling academy, and one by one, three of my sisters followed me. Now four of us are here, training together,' she said while preparing for the evening's warm-up session.

Surrounded by vibrant yellow mustard fields, the main building at the akhada was a modest, two-storey cement structure. The upper floor functioned as a hostel, with two rows of rooms furnished with bunk beds and steel almirahs. On the ground floor, an expansive hall, covered in wrestling mats and equipped with exercise gear, served as the training area.

For the girls in residence, life couldn't be more different between the two floors. The dormitory is friendly, the girls largely in groups of two or three, braiding hair, cooking comfort food on induction stoves, massaging sore limbs and watching videos on their phones.

On the mat, though, there are no friends – only players. Downstairs at Yudhveer Akhada, in the training hall, the same girls regarded each other as rivals whose strengths were to be as keenly noted as their vulnerabilities.

The first technique newcomers learn at an akhada is how to build a stance. A wrestler, as any coach will tell you, is as strong as their stance. It is the position they assume at the start of a bout: crouching, one leg at an angle to the other, one arm bent while the other is held straight out. For hours each day, a young wrestler holds this stance on the mat, mastering the art of strength in stillness.

As Prarthna took photographs, I stood in the doorway watching the school-age girls with taut muscles and intense focus lock in bouts across the length of the hall. One of the trainers broke down the techniques on display. A girl using the 'ankle pick' had grabbed her opponent's ankles while simultaneously pushing her upper body in an attempt to knock her off balance. Another had dived in for the 'double-leg takedown', wrapping both arms around the opponent's legs and pulling them in while shooting forward with her weight. Behind her, someone was in the middle of a 'fireman's carry', having ducked under her opponent's arm and secured it with one of her legs. She then lifted the opponent onto her shoulders, spun in a full circle, and slammed her down onto the mat. Soon after, a loud bell signalled the end of the three-hour session.

At the start of 2023, a group of Indian wrestlers launched a sit-in protest at Delhi's Jantar Mantar, a designated protest site, demanding the removal of Brij Bhushan Sharan Singh, then president of the Wrestling Federation of India (WFI). The wrestlers accused Singh of sexual harassment and sought his resignation, followed by legal action. Singh has repeatedly denied the allegations.

Sakshi Malik publicly shared her own experience of abuse. As a budding wrestler, she had endured years of harassment, from unwanted phone calls to an attempted assault just after she won her first gold medal at the Asian Junior Championships in Kazakhstan. Back in Almaty, in 2012, she did not lodge a formal complaint. Few girls did. Some were deterred by the formidable list of other criminal charges standing against Singh, which include murder and rioting, charges that he brandished as a badge of honour; others feared his rumoured capacity for vengeance, which had ended many a fledgling career. Brij Bhushan Sharan Singh ran Indian wrestling as a personal empire, and also wielded enormous political influence as a prominent leader of the Bharatiya Janata Party (BJP) and a six-time Member of Parliament, with close ties to powerful figures in Narendra Modi's government.

'We told each other: we have to fight without worrying about the result – like we do in wrestling,' Sakshi told me. Seated beside her in the tent at Jantar Mantar was Vinesh Phogat and her cousin, Sangeeta, also an award-winning wrestler. While dressed in their usual athletic wear, they tied black bands around their heads and arms to signal their new role as activists.

By this point, women wrestlers had collectively won dozens of coveted medals for India across international competitions. Their achievements had inspired a new generation of girls to take up wrestling, and they felt it was time to reform the system that had failed them and countless others. 'I did not want younger wrestlers to go through the same ordeal that I had to endure,' Sakshi told me. 'We had put everything on the line to sit in protest.'

For over forty days, they spent most of their time on the yellow tarpaulin resembling a wrestling mat – sitting, standing, sleeping, and sloganeering. With no prior experience in protesting, they were learning something new every day. Practically sleeping on the street, they were besieged by mosquitoes – a relentless swarm that multiplied at night. They covered themselves from head to toe as they slept, wearing thick socks on their feet, lest an exposed toe lure the insects. When unseasonal showers drenched their mattresses, they squeezed foldable cots through the police barricades. And when the police cut the electricity, they arranged for a generator to keep their loudspeakers running.

On 28 May 2023, they marched towards central Delhi, where Modi's government was set to inaugurate a new parliament building. Police personnel stormed the rally. 'There were several hands grabbing at me,' Sakshi Malik recalls in her memoir. 'I am sure they had plenty of experience with this sort of thing, but I was an Olympic medallist, after all. It is hard to drag me out of position.' With orders to arrest her, a group of policewomen tried to haul her into a bus where they had detained other protesters, but Sakshi, drawing on her practice of maintaining stance, stood her ground. The police won, after one of them got the idea to tickle her. 'My strength evaporated, and before I knew it, I was bundled into the bus.'

A procession of buses took the group to a police station, where they spent the night in detention. Released the next day, they announced a temporary suspension of their protest, assured by the sports minister of an investigation against Singh and fair elections to appoint the WFI's new governing committee.

After seven female wrestlers filed First Information Reports against Singh, the government suspended him from the post. But when the elections were announced months later, the sports ministry allowed Singh's close associate to contest the president's position. 'He was from the ruling party, so they had to side with him,' Sakshi told me.

His proxy candidate, Sanjay Singh, won the ballot, crushing any hope of accountability or reform.

Devastated, Sakshi Malik quit the sport. She had planned to retire after another shot at Olympic gold, with the ceremonial gesture of leaving her wrestling shoes at the edge of the mat. Instead, at a press conference in December 2023, she placed a pair of shoes she had been wearing on the table before her. Both she and Vinesh had tears in their eyes.

Though defeated in her protest, Vinesh decided to compete in the selection trials for the upcoming Olympics, aware that the ad hoc committee appointed by the government to oversee selections could make it difficult for her to go to Paris. Her fears were soon realised. The committee did not hold trials for the 53 kg category, instead choosing to send another wrestler, one who had fought in the same weight class in the last big competition – while Vinesh was protesting at Jantar Mantar. She reduced her weight to compete in the 50 kg trials, even though she naturally weighed up to five kilos more, and won.

She made it to Paris, proving her mettle as an athlete at the top of her game. But before her final match for Olympic gold, she was disqualified after she weighed in 100 g above 50 kg. She had taken extreme measures to keep herself at the requisite weight – going as far as standing upside down in a sauna and letting blood – but it was not enough.

Back in India, the news reached thousands of fans who had stayed up to witness what might have been a historic match. Vinesh's previous performances in Paris had been exceptional. One highlight was her victory over Japan's Yui Susaki in the opening round – a landmark win, as Susaki, a four-time world champion, had remained undefeated on the international stage. For the most part, Phogat focused on defence, skilfully neutralising Susaki's attacks through arm clinches and head-to-head resistance. With approximately seven seconds remaining, she executed a swift takedown. She lunged at

Susaki and, before her opponent could react, flipped her onto the mat, using her weight to pin her down while her hands encircled her from beneath, securing two points.

Had she been allowed to compete in her usual weight class, she might have won the final match too. Her Olympic journey served as a stark reminder that politics can eclipse even the finest talent in any arena, including professional sports.

This competition was to be the 29-year-old's last. 'I don't have any more strength now. Goodbye wrestling, 2001–2024,' she posted on her social media pages.

In May, a Delhi court framed charges against Singh for sexual harassment and intimidation, among other offences. The trial is currently under way, with witness testimonies being recorded.

Sakshi now trains aspiring wrestlers at her father-in-law's academy in Rohtak, her home town. She told me the younger generation will have to continue the fight they began. 'I tell them it is not enough to master the techniques. It is equally important to raise one's voice against injustice.'

Vinesh, just weeks after returning from Paris, joined the Indian National Congress, the BJP's main opposition. By September she was standing as the party's candidate in regional elections in Haryana, her home state. The seat she contested, Julana, had never before seen a woman candidate in the race for the state assembly.

Vinesh approached politics like a sportsperson, embracing the challenge. On her first major campaign day, she ran an impromptu foot race among party members and supporters – she came first. Her election pitch focused on the rights of farmers, sportspersons, and young people. Part of her agenda, she explained, was to give young athletes the confidence that someone was standing up for them.

On 8 October, as the votes were being counted, she initially trailed behind the BJP candidate, but eventually she took the lead, winning by 6,015 votes.

Afterwards, addressing the press, she declared her win belonged to 'every girl, every woman who chooses the path of struggle'. For the first time in a long while, Vinesh Phogat was smiling. ■

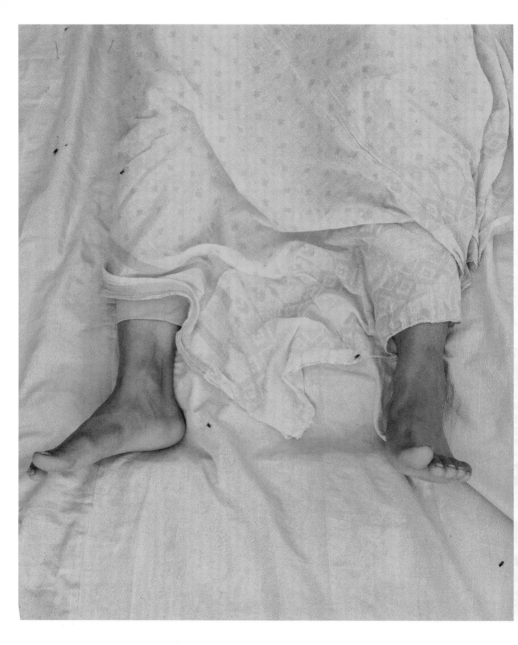

SYBREN VANOVERBERGHE
Red Facade, 2019
Courtesy of Keteleer Gallery

THE DANCE

Mircea Cărtărescu

TRANSLATED FROM THE ROMANIAN BY SEAN COTTER

In the course of my countless journeys through the archipelago, I once encountered an island surrounded by green waters, hexagons of light dancing in the sun. The land was pale in comparison with the litharge of those seas, and with the wings of giant albatrosses sliding across the immaculate sky, the scene would have enchanted any human eye. You could only wonder whether that craggy place was not home to the untouched palace that the diminutive locals, with their fezzes of brick-red felt and stilettos in their cummerbunds, spoke of during the hour of siesta, while you squatted beside a wall and dragged on a shisha. There were, they said, many chambers in the palace, full of unknown wonders, but it was not these that merited risking your life, not these that were worth the trouble, to write a story with a needle in the corner of your eye. Rather, in the center of the palace was the Exit, blocked by a ferocious guardian, whom none could pass. No one had ever vanquished him, and the defeated warriors returned wizened and raw. What was beyond the Exit no one knew, but the angels who occasionally descended to the islands, be it to bless a procession of tear-stained icons, or to rebuke a fool who slept with his wife while she was unclean, or to run various other errands, told of a depth as endless as the ocean floor littered with shattered wooden boats, their holds filled with treasure, and surrounded by fish with pointed beaks, and octopi, and ancient statues of marble flesh.

Any sailor, it was said, might reach that island once in his life, guided by the zodiac charts consulted at his birth. I was thus not surprised that, at the age of fifty – when a man whose skin has been thickened by salt and storms is drawn toward home – it was given to me to place my foot on the burning sands of that storied island. I was not afraid, nor was I pleased: thus it had to be, as I always told myself when facing a new day, a new woman, a new stranger with my knife in his chest. One cannot do anything but what heaven compels. In a man's last moment, he regards his life and understands: thus it had to be.

I made land on a dinghy, leaving the barque a hundred cubits' distance from the rocks. The sun was high, I saw no shadow. Fig trees grew wild, full of violet fruits. In the middle of the island was a ring of cliffs, as slim and irregular as a giant's teeth. With much effort, I found the narrow through which I could penetrate. And there, rising between the rocks, with yellow walls bracing an arched cupola in the shape of a skull, was the palace built by inhuman hands. I entered it as much in search of shade as of adventure, the sun having become blistering, and my clothes and hair were soaked with sweat as though I had swum there. In the vast halls I found shadow, much shadow, thick shadow, of the highest quality.

The palace was immense and deserted, its walls covered with arabesques. In the interior courtyards, fountains lay still, their waters long since evaporated. In their spiral basins, spiders wove dusty cobwebs. The halls were lined with doors; I opened as many as I could. Each led into a chamber with a window facing the sea. Each had a stone cube in its center, where a baffling machinery churned, a golden fish flapped, suspended in a crystal sphere, or a girl sat with her feet hanging, her face sulking at me, like a strange fruit of the sea, wearing a breastplate of rose ivory. Another chamber held a lobster the size of a large dog; it pinched beads of water between its claws and regarded me with blind eyes.

There were more and more halls, but soon I stopped investigating the closed doors, abandoning the surprises that might have been waiting in the chambers behind them, because I was impatient to stand before the Exit. I advanced for hours over the gentle tiles of polished stone. Here and there I passed large, symmetrical openings in the exterior walls, where I saw the sky and sea on every side. Pelicans rested on long ledges, peering inside with one red eye, but not daring to violate the shadow with their flight. Just when I began to lose faith in the stories of the island and to ruminate a return to my ship, I passed through a high arch of porphyry that led into the chamber of the great portal. The chamber was perfectly round, and in its perimeter I counted eleven entrances like this one, buried in the same scarlet stone. The opposite doors could barely be seen across the room's immensity. I reckoned I was in the palace center, under the skull-like dome visible from the shore, and which, now I marveled, had its hemispheric ceiling painted with the volutes of a brain – the living and mortal throne of the human soul.

In the precise center of the room something flashed like lightning. A perpendicular column of pure light descended from the large round hole at the apex of the cupola, a sign that the sun stood constantly above the island. Flickering in the distance was the portal; its flames blinded me as I approached the central depth of the chamber with my arm across my eyes. In this same posture, once in the days of my youth, had I thrown myself from the ship's prow into the flashing ocean, in the center of its roundness, and swam toward the sun on its path of fire and water, the rays and wetness quivering in ever-changing proportions.

When I reached the Exit I was so stunned my heart stopped, because at the same moment, as though waiting for me since the beginnings of the world, from the depths of the Exit appeared the guardian. Now we stared at each other fiercely, determined to stand our ground. He had sworn an oath to the gods to repel intruders, even at the price of his life, and I was constant in my desire to know what lay beyond, and my will was equal to any oath, and any god. We stood face-to-face, with the portal between us, our eyes glaring at the other ferociously.

The guardian was a hearty man about fifty. A scar, similar to the one that furrowed my left temple, also furrowed his, but on the right side. His clothes matched mine, but he was evidently left-handed, because he wore his hilt on his right hip. His boots had perhaps been made by the same bootmaker as worked mine, but then he had mistaken the two initials of his name, printed near the top of the leather: the guardian's were strangely reversed.

I took a step forward, and he did as well. I attempted to pass him, and he blocked my way, rushing toward the side where I advanced. I shoved him and he shoved me, with his hands braced against my own. Scarlet with fury, I drew my dagger from my waistband and he drew his own at the same moment. I aimed the tip of my blade at his heart and – who will believe me? Who could believe in curses and magic? – our blades met in the middle at their finest tips, as had never before happened and could never happen. I threw my weapon onto the floor, convinced it would be of no use, and he did the same, perhaps relying more on the diabolical power of his spells and charms.

We stood face-to-face, two men huffing with the weight of their years, looking hopelessly at each other. I rose again, reengaged the battle with all my power – but to no end. It was as though he had a thousand hands and a hundred bodies. His bearded head, his broad chest, his large belly, his sculpted thighs filled every corner of the Exit's shimmering expanse. Hour after hour passed in clenches, huffing, groans and sweat, our bellows cast against and resounding from the chamber's distant walls.

I faced the guardian, who had exhausted all his previous adversaries, and I searched for a way to prove myself more cunning than he. I studied his movements. I dropped my head and looked at him through my eyebrows, and he did precisely the same. But if I leaned to the right, he leaned to the left, remaining my opposite. I leaned forward, and he did the same. I raised my left arm, he his right. I put my hand over my heart: his heart was on the right! The monster only appeared to be human, under his skin he was inverted, as the left hand is to the right. I stood again before the Exit – the only one in our world, as the all-knowing and tight-lipped women had told me in the fruit market – and I leaned my chest against his, my eyes on his eyes, my mouth on his mouth, my hands and feet on his hands and feet, pressing with all my might against his strong and immobile body. We pressed our foreheads against each other until our browbones were bruised.

I could not pass. My amazement knew no bounds. I had expected a hard battle with the omnipotent guardian, I had thought that in the end I would writhe in my own blood, but such direct and stubborn opposition completely disoriented me. I was about the same stature as he: why couldn't I send him to one side so I could finally pass beyond him? Was it my fate never to see the treasures of the sunken galleys, the pale statues, the deceitful glints of the depths?

I stayed there for days on end, first looking for a crack in the defense of the terrible guardian, then lying on the floor resigned, and then overwhelmed with fury and kicking and punching against the ever-potent refusals of his feet and hands, then again hopeless, stretched over the floor . . . I sat one evening on the cool tiles, and he did the same. I lay my entire body on the floor, and bracing my chin in my hands, I pondered until I felt my mind would explode. The brave guardian was obviously as strong as I was. Bodily vigor had proven pointless, I would not get rid of him but through some ruse, which I should devise as quickly as possible.

Through the large, azure opening in the peak of the cupola, swarms of angels constantly descended, bathed in light, as irritating as mosquitoes. They gathered around me, they offered asinine advice, they spoke of dogmas and mysteries, they bored me with their ashen faces that knew neither laughter nor tears. Others, identical and evasive, perched on the sills along the chamber's narrow windows, dangling their legs inside, written like icons in two types of blue, that of the sea below and that of the sky above.

Angels, in that summer, had infested the entire archipelago. In other years there had been harpies, and before that there were soft, transparent rocks that would swallow a man whole, and then spit out his bones only a few moments later. The old people remembered the depraved women of the sea, who in ancient times emerged from the foamy waves to show the fisherman, in an extended palm, their lemon-like eggs, each with a person crouched inside. And each tiny person resembled the fisherman and called him Father, begging him to take them home to his earthen hut. The angels were not the worst infestation the archipelago had periodically experienced, but they were the most insufferable, harping on endlessly: thou shalt not steal, thou shalt not murder, thou shalt not covet your neighbor's wife . . . The old tars often claimed the man-eating stones were more humane. Now the angels sat like pelicans on the windowsills, twisting their heads to either side, perhaps laying bets on the eventual victor, because I often saw, from the corner of my eye, the flash of coins being flipped in the air and dexterously caught with a smack of the right palm on the back of the left. 'Heads,' some shouted, 'Tails,' said others, but I could not guess the battle's denouement until one of them shouted loud enough to echo through the dome, in agony or in triumph. He had driven his coin, which in the air resembled a dandelion tuft, impetuously into the flesh of his left hand, where it had landed on its edge. He could just make out the ridges, like those of a giant fish, on the back of his bloody hand. When I heard the unlucky angel's cry, like a wounded bird, I received a blessed thought from on high.

Heaven's stars do not bestow on us, we human beings, merely resilience and courage; they also give wisdom. Often a small and nimble ship, with well-sewn sails, may sink the heavy galleon that vainly blasts its cannons at flies. I remembered one afternoon the story of a muezzin, on one of these islands, who only descended from his minaret to milk his goats. He had heard, and told the same to others, that in the wilds of other lands, a small creature resembling a weasel bested the great hooded snake with a wondrously devious tactic: face-to-face with the giant serpent, overshadowed by its hood, this creature of God called the mongoose began to dance, up and down, side to side, while the evil worm did the same, its head raised and tail twisted into the dust. To and fro, left and right, to and fro, left and right, to and fro . . . always the same and ever faster, until the snake came to believe that it knew, a moment ahead, what its enemy would do. When the speed reached the point you could barely see the two heads moving together, the mongoose suddenly changed its movement: instead of right, it went left, and the reptile, leaning to the opposite side, for a brief moment revealed its neck. In a flash it pounced onto the snake's back and killed it with a cry of victory.

This idea reinvigorated me. I leapt in that moment to my feet and once again moved toward the great Exit, the only one in our world. As I fully expected, the guardian appeared, determined and also reinvigorated, from his hellish hole. I stood a few moments without moving, pondering my tactic, assembling my plan from forty steps, in the six directions in which the human mind can think: forward, back, left, right, leap, crouch. Difficult to learn, but easy to remember (because the steps repeated in a delicate order whose import slowly came clear), my dance was as symmetrical and subtle as a spider's web. When I lifted my eyes, I met his gaze and thought I saw a chill flash through his body. Taking one step to the left, I began, as slowly as in a dream, the deadly dance, the final dance, the dance of all dances.

I laid, ten times in a row, the trap of steps, each time slightly faster than before. Then another ten times. And another. The monster came forward, moved back, leaned his body to the right and to the left without mistake, he leapt and crouched at the same moment I did, with the precision of an astrolabe. I started the series of movements again, with re-energized speed, until I thought my shoulders would pop from their sockets and my knees would split apart. After the fortieth identical repetition, heated as though enveloped by flames, I made the first foreign movement. Sudden and bewildering, as though I had grown an extra hand, or my body had grown an extra body. But the monster made no mistake. At the same time, in the same split second, he also turned from the beaten path, following the unknown. We found ourselves again chest-to-chest, we saw our eyes again full of hate, we broke our fists on the other's fists, our screams echoing the other's screams.

I began again, with the strength of ten men. I laid the trap hundreds and thousands of times. I suddenly changed my movement in so many ways and at so many different moments that the change itself became part of the dance, just as easy to predict as the trap's forty steps. For that reason, perhaps, the guardian never made a mistake, however deft my movements. One thousand times, one million times, more times than grains of sand and more than all the tears the world has ever shed, I started the dance over again, without understanding that I had been caught in my own trap and that I danced a petty, fruitless dance that would lead to no victory.

When I suddenly understood what the angels had shouted, that battle is not battle but a dance without beginning, without end, and without limit, I gave up on the trap and the mongoose stratagem. I forgot about the guardian and did nothing other than live in the eternal fire of the dance, with no goal, with no desire, with no memory. I danced with all my might, I danced with twenty hearts and eight arms, I danced with thousands of feet, I danced with the six dimensions that grew from my kidneys and time's lance emerging from below my left breast. I didn't dance, rather I was danced, I merely placed my hands and feet inside the hands and feet of the dance. With my body, my strings of guts, my veins, my blood and my bile, with my spine I filled the entire chamber of the great portal, leaving not even the point of a needle unfilled with blood, sperm, teeth and nails, with thousands of eyes and thousands of ears and thousands of fingers and thousands of lips. I danced the Archimedian spiral, I danced the golden ratio, I danced the Fibonacci sequence, I danced the Lie groups, I danced the sacred dance of quaternions and octonions. I danced the genesis of space on the Planck scale and the birth of time in causation, and the hideous screams of Bekenstein scales and the 10^{500} possible, impossible, probable, improbable universes, and the dust of galaxies from Laniakea, the dust of dust of dust of galaxies, the dust of dust of dust of worlds . . . I danced the eternal flame, its eternal return of spark and snuff, furiously consuming the logical space of the mind. I danced the melted gold icon of the Godhead.

As I danced to one side and the other of the Exit, I was the portal, I was the guardian, I was the wheel of angels, I was the palace, I was the sea. The brain, heart and sex, so often pitted against each other, were now a single organ, whose thought flowed into sensation, sensation into pleasure, and pleasure back into thought, and everything broke through my skin and poured into the skin of the world, and broke through and poured, wastelaying and torrential and unstoppable, into the icon of the All, which it also broke through to pour itself into the eternal and ineffable Nothing.

When the dance finished, I found myself again on the threshold of the great portal. Beyond it now was no one. But I could not find within me any reason left to enter. I turned back and crossed the chamber again, under the eyes of angels in the windows, I left through the porphyry archway, I retread the long corridors, without the desire to open a single door. I came into the steady sunlight of the afternoon, crossing the ring of cliffs, passing beside the fig trees with violet fruits to reach my dinghy perched on the shore. The archipelago with its glassy sea, blazing against my sight, with its forested coastlands, seemed to me beauties beyond our power to express. I reached my ship ready to pull the sea air into my chest, my skin wizened by salt and storms. And this is what I have done until today, because this is man's fate on earth. At some moment I will turn homeward, but not as long as I feel a trace of life left within me. And with my last breath, I hope I will be able to say to myself, in peace, with my hand on my right breast, over my heart, unafraid: thus it had to be. ∎

CONTRIBUTORS

Myriam Boulos is a photographer from Lebanon. In 2021, she joined Magnum as a nominee. Her book, *What's Ours*, was published by Aperture in 2023.

Clare Bucknell is the author of *The Treasuries: Poetry Anthologies and the Making of British Culture* (2023). She writes for the *London Review of Books* and the *New York Review of Books*.

Mircea Cărtărescu was born in Bucharest, where he still lives. His work has been translated into multiple languages and includes *Nostalgia, Blinding, Solenoid, Melancolia* and most recently *Theodoros*.

Tereza Červeňová is a visual artist working with photography. *Nymph*, her new book, documents her two-year Warburg Institute art residency, intertwining the building's transformation with themes of visibility, vulnerability and women's shared journey in claiming space.

Caryl Churchill is the playwright of *Top Girls, Far Away, A Number, Love and Information, Glass. Kill.*

Bluebeard. Imp., Cloud Nine, Serious Money and *What If If Only*.

Sean Cotter is the translator of many works of Romanian literature, most recently Mircea Cărtărescu's *Solenoid* (2021), and the author of *Literary Translation and the Idea of a Minor Romania* (2014; and in Dana Bădulescu's translation, 2024).

Owen Hatherley is the author of several books, most recently *Transitional Objects* and *Walking the Streets/Walking the Projects*. *The Alienation Effect*, a book about Central European migrant artists and intellectuals in twentieth-century Britain, will be published in March 2025. He is a contributing editor at *Jacobin*.

An-My Lê is a photographer primarily based in New York. Her work often addresses the impact of war on culture and the environment, and has been exhibited in the Whitney Biennial, the Metropolitan Museum of Art and the Tate Modern.

Benjamin Nugent is the author of *Fraternity: Stories* (2020). His fiction has appeared in the *Atlantic*, *Best American Short Stories* and the *Paris Review*.

K Patrick is a poet and fiction writer based in Scotland. Their debut novel, *Mrs S*, was published in 2023, and their poetry collection, *Three Births*, in 2024.

Snigdha Poonam is a journalist based in India and the UK. Her first book, *Dreamers: How Young Indians Are Changing the World*, was published in 2018.

Declan Ryan's first collection of poems, *Crisis Actor*, was published in 2023.

Edward Salem is the author of the forthcoming books *Intifadas* (2026) and *Monk Fruit* (2025). His work has appeared in the *New York Review of Books*, *Poetry* and the *Kenyon Review*.

Prarthna Singh's book, *Har Shaam Shaheen Bagh*, was self-published in 2022. Her work has appeared in *TIME*, the *New York Times* and the *Economist*. She has exhibited at Rencontres d'Arles, Photo Saint Germain and the National Portrait Gallery.

Kathryn Scanlan is the author of *The Dominant Animal*, *Kick the Latch* and *Aug 9—Fog*, a new edition of which will be published this year by Book Works in the UK.

Nico Walker is the author of the novel *Cherry* (2018). He lives in New York City with his wife.

GRANTA TRUST

Granta would be unable to fulfil its mission
without the generosity of its donors.

We gratefully acknowledge the following
individuals and foundations:

Ford Foundation
British Council
Jerwood Foundation
Pulitzer Center
Amazon Literary Partnership
Sigrid Rausing
The Hans and Marit Rausing Charitable Trust
Anonymous
Bloomsbury Publishing Plc
SALT
Open Society
The Common Humanity Arts Trust

If you would like to contribute, please make
a donation at granta.com/donate.

The Granta Writers Workshop

NATURE WRITING, SHORT FICTION, LONG-FORM JOURNALISM, MEMOIR

'One purpose of art is to get us to wake up, recalibrate our emotional life, get ourselves into proper relation to reality.'
– GEORGE SAUNDERS

Image © Julie Cockburn

Congratulations to the 2024 winners of the
Whiting Creative Nonfiction Grant

Apply now through April 23, 2025 at whiting.org/nonfiction

The Whiting Creative Nonfiction Grant of $40,000 is awarded to writers in the process of completing a work of nonfiction to the highest aesthetic and intellectual level. It is intended to encourage original and ambitious projects by giving its grantees the additional means to do exacting research and devote time to composition.

To be eligible, books must be under contract with a publisher in Canada, the UK, or US. Read more or sign up for an information session at whiting.org/nonfiction

whiting
FOUNDATION

Leah Broad
This Woman's War: Women and Music in World War II

James Duesterberg
Final Fantasy: A Secret History of the Present

Arun Kundnani
I Rise in Fire: H. Rap Brown, Jamil Al-Amin, and the Long Revolution

Sarah Esther Maslin
Nothing Stays Buried: Trauma, Truth, and One Town's Fight for Justice in the Aftermath of a Massacre

Hettie O'Brien
Diminishing Returns

Emily Ogden
Frailties: How Poe Helps Us Live with Ourselves

Nadim Roberts
The Highway

Heather Ann Thompson
Fear and Fury: Bernhard Goetz and the Rebirth of White Vigilantism in America

Ronald Williams II
Black Embassy: TransAfrica and the Struggle for Foreign Policy Justice

Hannah Zeavin
All Freud's Children: A Story of Inheritance